Inventions

A VISUAL HISTORY

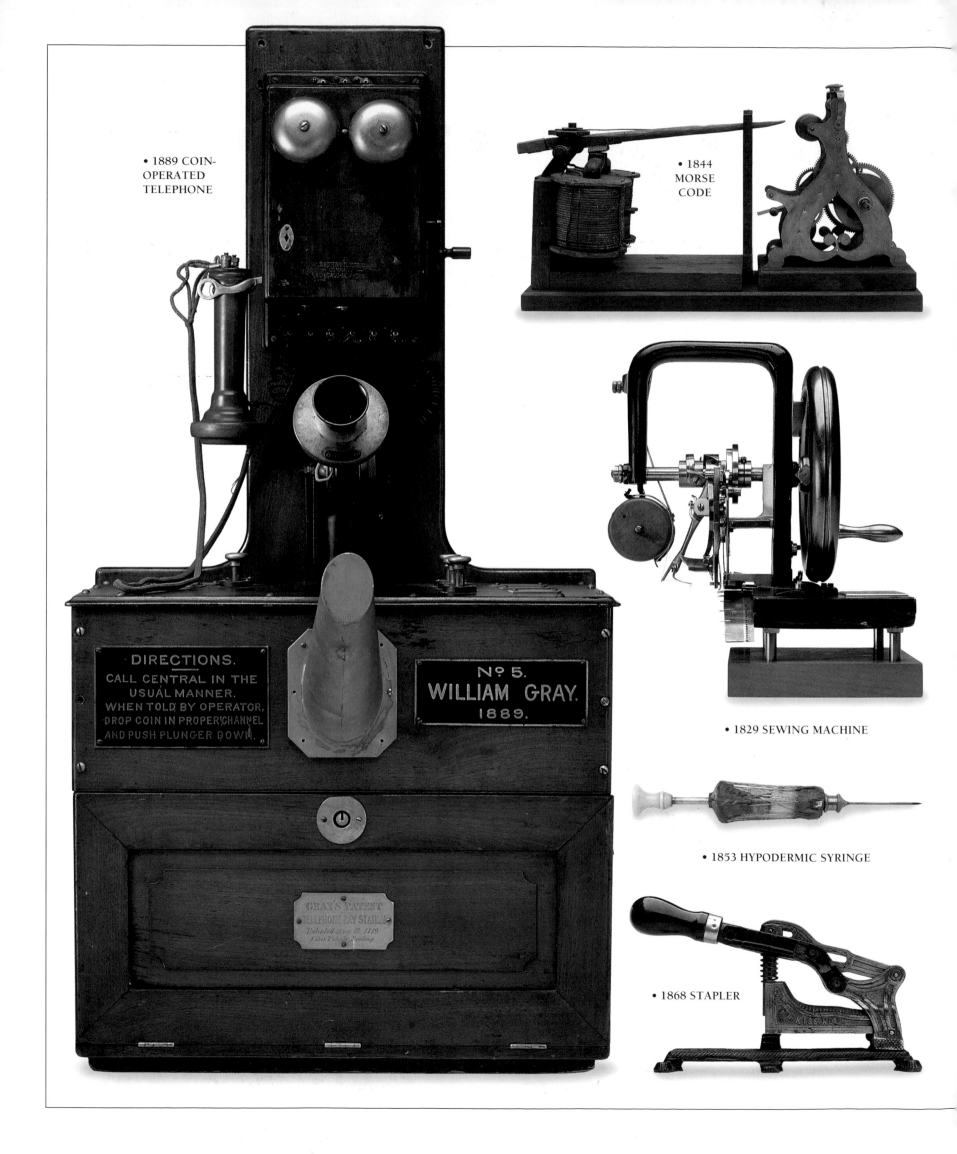

• 1889 COIN-OPERATED TELEPHONE

• 1844 MORSE CODE

DIRECTIONS.
CALL CENTRAL IN THE USUAL MANNER.
WHEN TOLD BY OPERATOR, DROP COIN IN PROPER CHANNEL AND PUSH PLUNGER DOWN.

No 5.
WILLIAM GRAY.
1889.

• 1829 SEWING MACHINE

• 1853 HYPODERMIC SYRINGE

• 1868 STAPLER

Inventions
A VISUAL HISTORY

RICHARD PLATT

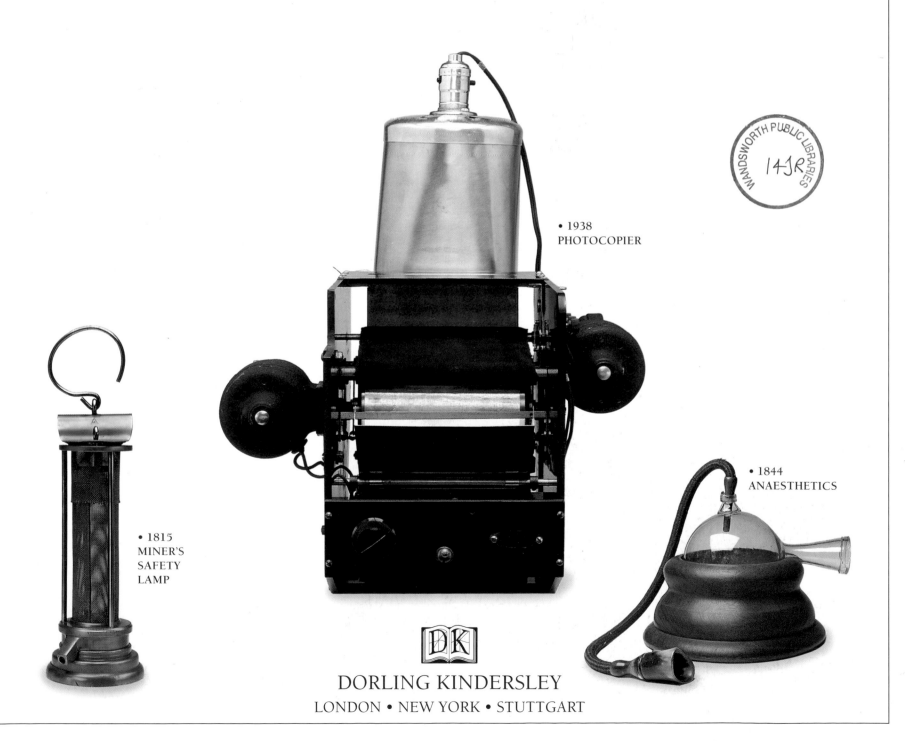

• 1938
PHOTOCOPIER

• 1815
MINER'S
SAFETY
LAMP

• 1844
ANAESTHETICS

DK

DORLING KINDERSLEY

LONDON • NEW YORK • STUTTGART

A DORLING KINDERSLEY BOOK

Project Editor Anderley Moore

Art Editor Tina Neville

Managing Editor Helen Parker

Managing Art Editor Peter Bailey

Picture Research Caroline Brooke

Production Louise Barratt

Editorial Consultants Eryl Davies
Susan Watt

SMITHSONIAN INSTITUTION PRESS
BOOK DEVELOPMENT DIVISION

Executive Editor Caroline Newman

Editor Heidi M. Lumberg

Picture Editors Paula Dailey
Anne K. DuVivier

SMITHSONIAN INSTITUTION REVIEW PANEL
NATIONAL MUSEUM OF AMERICAN HISTORY

Ramunas Kondratas, Peter Liebhold,
Steven Lubar, and Deborah Warner

First published in Great Britain in 1994 by Dorling
Kindersley Limited, 9 Henrietta Street,
London WC2E 8PS

300523263

2/95

JR
609
PLAT

A CIP catalogue record for this book is available
from the British Library

ISBN 07513 5225X

Reproduced by Colourscan, Singapore

Printed and bound in Italy by
A. Mondadori Editore, Verona

Contents

Foreword

GREAT INVENTIONS ARE REVOLUTIONARY IDEAS that change the world. The people who first invented a way of making fire were able to venture far from home without fear of the cold. The invention of radio brought distant places closer together. Some inventions, though, just make life more comfortable or enjoyable – like musical instruments, or clothes dyes. In the pages that follow, you'll find all kinds of inventions, from the world-changing to the trivial.

But what exactly is an invention? It's a new and better way of doing something: a tool to make a job easier; a farming method that feeds more mouths for less effort; a sharper weapon that gives a warrior a fighting advantage; or a construction technique for making bigger buildings.

Not every good idea leads to a practical application. Italian genius Leonardo da Vinci first scribbled ideas for chains to drive machines during the 15th-century – but the technology to produce them did not exist. Chain-driven machines were not practical for another four centuries. In 1885, John Kemp Starley fitted a chain and wire-spoked wheels – neither of which he invented – to the original 1839 bicycle. His *innovation* (improvement) transformed the bike from a dangerous novelty to a practical and safe form of transport. A great invention, then, may be unworkable until it is combined with several other good ideas.

The subtle difference between invention and innovation often makes it difficult to know who to name as inventor. But this is just one of many problems in assigning credit. History itself acts like a distorting mirror, twisting or hiding the truth. Often people take the credit for an invention simply because they were the first to describe it: Archimedes, for instance, almost certainly did not invent the screw-shaped water-lifting tube that bears his name.

Prejudice clouds the picture, too. Until recently, historians favoured European inventors because they found it hard to accept the idea of African or Chinese ingenuity. Printing is a fine example of this misrepresentation: German artisans usually take the credit for the invention of printing in the 15th century, yet Asian printers were using moveable type four centuries earlier.

I've tried to present the fairest, fullest, and most accurate picture of the story of invention. However, technology does not advance at a convenient, steady rate. Sometimes a rush of ingenuity and invention means there just isn't enough space on the page to tell the full story of every invention exactly where it belongs. So, if your favourite invention isn't at the date where you expect it, look on: you may find it listed under the year the patent was filed, or when a great but impractical idea first became a useful, working product.

Richard Platt

600,000 BC–AD 1299
The first inventions

THE STORY OF INVENTION – and of human history itself – begins with the first stone tools made by our ancestors more than two million years ago. The ability to create tools is one of the key differences between apes and the human species. Perhaps the most important discovery was in the Olduvai Gorge, Tanzania, East Africa, where, in 1960, the remains of a human-like skeleton were found, surrounded by animal bones and simple stone choppers and scrapers. This early human was fittingly called *Homo habilis*, meaning "handy man" in Latin.

These first Africans probably used their stone tools to kill and butcher animals for food. This improved their diet and gave them an advantage over their neighbours, who did not have the stone-tool technology. *Homo habilis* thrived, gradually growing over thousands of years in both height and intelligence to become *Homo erectus* – "upright man".

But the process of invention was slow to begin with. It was another five hundred thousand years after the first stone tools were used that early people invented ways of making and using fire to improve their lives.

Who did what?

Before the existence of written records, our knowledge of invention is based solely on what archaeologists can piece together from the past. By studying the buried remains of human societies, we can date early inventions and guess where their inventors lived. But what if these remains are not the first? It is a mistake to assume that the most inventive ancient

Pebble tool, found in the Olduvai Gorge in Tanzania

THE FIRST TOOLS

The very first tools dating back two million years are the Oldowan tools found in the Olduvai Gorge in Tanzania, Africa. Over a million years, early hominids refined their tool-making skills and by around one million years ago, they had perfected the stone handaxe.

FLINT WORKING

Flint core is trimmed to a rough tool shape.

A large chip is removed from the underside using a stone hammer.

Handaxe from Egypt, made by an early hominid – before humans had fully evolved

The axe is trimmed with a bone hammer.

THE CHANGING WORLD: 600,000 BC–AD 1299

FIRE-MAKING
The invention of fire-making tools meant that early people could protect themselves from wild animals and survive in colder climates. Fire also allowed them to cook and eat foods that were indigestible when raw, and metalworking would have been impossible without it.

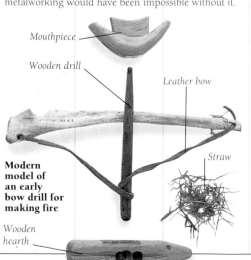

Mouthpiece
Wooden drill
Leather bow

Modern model of an early bow drill for making fire

Wooden hearth

Straw

FARMING
With the invention of methods of irrigation, the plough, sickle, and domestication of animals, hunter-gatherers gradually gave up their wandering way of life and settled to become farmers. Crops were cultivated, and people learned ways of making flour from grain. This change in lifestyle eventually led to towns, cities, and the emergence of a "civilized" society.

Seeds are placed on the mortar.

Mortar and pestle, c.1200 BC

Pestle is used to grind seeds.

BUILDING
New techniques for building domes and arches and the invention of set squares and plumb lines enabled people to make bigger, stronger buildings. This detail from the Trajan Column in Rome (AD 113) shows Roman builders at work.

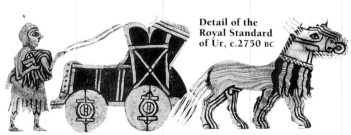

Detail of the Royal Standard of Ur, c.2750 BC

LAND TRANSPORT
The invention of the wheel and the domestication of animals made it possible to transport heavy goods over long distances.

peoples are those whose remains we can see. The dry climate of Egypt has preserved the world's earliest pictures of sailing boats, painted between five and six thousand years ago, but what about the sailing vessels used by the peoples of the Pacific? We know that they moved from island to island at about the same time, or even earlier, yet no trace remains of the boats in which they must surely have navigated a path across the ocean.

The rise of civilization

Technology began to move forward more quickly with the rise of agriculture, trade, and social organization. As early people learned how to cultivate crops and domesticate animals they gave up their wandering, hunter-gatherer lifestyle. Farming settlements grew up along the world's great rivers: the Nile, the Tigris and the Euphrates, the Indus, and the Huang He (Yellow River). Here, the fertile soil meant enough food could be produced to support larger populations. People began to develop craft skills to make pottery, tools, and weapons as well as luxury items, which were increasingly traded with neighbouring groups.

In time, societies developed more clearly defined government structures, and the first towns and cities emerged. Loosely organized hunting groups evolved into armies, and technology and invention turned to supplying military needs. New weapons made wars more deadly, and many smaller civilizations were conquered by powerful neighbours to create immense, wealthy empires. The invention of the wheel and the building of extensive trade networks allowed people to travel farther over land, while sail-powered boats guided by new navigational instruments opened up the ocean. As world trade flourished, so did invention. By the end of the 13th century AD, the foundations for all the modern technologies were already laid.

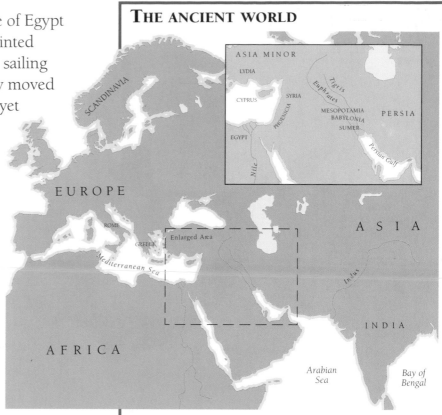

THE ANCIENT WORLD

IMPORTANT PEOPLES AND CIVILIZATIONS
The main areas of invention correspond with the first great civilizations, which were often situated in fertile river valleys.

Sumer 5000–2000 BC Southern Mesopotamia
Ancient Egypt 3000–1000 BC Egypt and the Nile valley
Babylonia 2800–1750 BC Lower Euphrates valley
Indus Valley 2500–1500 BC Indus river valley in India
Ancient Greece 2000–30 BC Greece and Asia Minor
Shang Dynasty 1650–1027 BC Northeast China
Lapita 1500 BC–AD 1200 Islands of the western Pacific
Zhou Dynasty 1027–771 BC Northeast China
Maya 1000 BC–AD 1697 Central America
Assyria 750–612 BC Mesopotamia and Nile valley
Persia 632–331 BC Egypt to Indus valley
Ancient Rome 200 BC–AD 400 Britain to the Persian Gulf
Vikings AD 700–900 Scandinavia and northern Europe

NEW MATERIALS
Once people could smelt and work metals such as bronze and eventually iron, they could make much stronger, more hard-wearing tools and weapons.

Chinese bronze vessel, c.1600 BC

Weather vane from the prow of a Viking ship, Norway

NAVIGATION AT SEA
The first oar-powered boats probably stayed close to land and found their way by following recognized points on the coast. The invention of sails to power boats made longer journeys possible, prompting sailors to learn how to plot their course across oceans by the position of the stars. The increasing number of sailing vessels led to an expansion in world trade, and in the size of the known world.

TRAVEL AND CONQUEST
The first horses and asses to be domesticated, around 6,000 years ago, were used in harness to draw wheeled carts and war chariots. Horse riding did not become common until the 8th century BC. After the invention of the saddle and stirrups in the 9th century AD, the nature of warfare changed as mass charges of cavalry armed with spears were easily able to defeat foot soldiers.

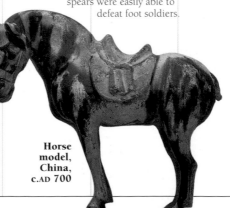

Horse model, China, c.AD 700

ENERGY SOURCES
Until the invention of ways of harnessing wind and water power, humans and animals had provided the power to grind grain into flour. Labour-saving water mills and windmills were used for centuries to power machines. This 15th-century scene shows both types of mill in use.

600,000 BC

50,000 BC

600,000 BC	490,000 BC	380,000 BC	270,000 BC	160,000 BC	50,000 BC	44,000 BC		26,000 BC

COUNTING & COMMUNICATION

Hide strap from which to suspend the lamp

Wick soaks up oil and keeps flame alive

Hollow shell holds reserves of oil

Oil lamp made from shell

c.45,000 BC PAINT
Weather and sunlight have erased most prehistoric paintings, but a few remain in the darkness of caves. The artists who painted these images of the beasts they hunted made black paint from charcoal or manganese oxide; for red they used iron oxide (rust); yellow paint came from iron carbonate. To make the pigments stick to the cave wall they mixed in animal fat, water, blood, or urine. And to store their colours they used shells and hollowed-out bones.

Prehistoric cave painting, Lascaux, France

DAILY LIFE & HEALTH

c.600,000 BC FIRE
The ability to use fire gave ancient people a greater chance of survival. With fire, they could keep warm and explore cooler regions. They used flames to protect themselves against dangerous animals or to drive them into traps. Fire also meant they could cook different foods. The first evidence of the use of fire comes from China. Layers of charcoal in caves at Choukoutien, near Beijing, show that the cave dwellers knew how to control fire, and how to keep it going by adding fuel, but there is no evidence of fire-making equipment until later.

c.50,000 BC OIL LAMP
Firebrands – burning branches – provided the first source of portable artificial light, but they soon burned down. The Stone-Age cave paintings of France would have been impossible without a better source of light. The people who created these paintings 25,000–50,000 years ago, probably worked by the dim light of a sputtering oil lamp. This was simply a lump of animal fat in a hollow stone or shell, with a wick made of moss. Though burn marks on cave walls and roofs show that lamps were used, no lamps survive from this date; the earliest, from the Grotte de la Mouthe in the Dordogne region of France, is about 17,000 years old.

c.30,000 BC FIRED CERAMICS
Objects moulded in wet clay keep their shape as the clay dries; but if the clay becomes wet again, it soon crumbles. By about 30,000 BC, during the last Ice Age, hunters in Moravia (now the Czech Republic) had learned how to harden clay permanently by firing, or heating it in a hearth. The first fired ceramics were clay models of animals. Potmaking was not invented for another 20,000 years.

AGRICULTURE & INDUSTRY

TRAVEL & CONQUEST

c.400,000 BC SPEAR
The earliest surviving example of a sharpened wooden pole, or spear, comes from Essex, England. Ancient hunters had sharpened the simple spear with a flint shaver. They must have been very brave – or perhaps foolhardy – for they used this simple tool to hunt mammoths. Singeing the spear-tip in a fire hardened the wood, making a more effective weapon. This technique was in use in Lehringen, near Bremen, Germany, around the same time: a complete spear was found inside a mammoth skeleton there.

c.250,000 BC AXE
The first shaped stone axes had no handles. They were roughly triangular, with one edge chipped sharp, and the other two smoothed for a more comfortable grip. Axes like these were a natural development from simple stone knives, and they have been found in the remains of ancient settlements in Africa, Europe, and Asia.

Axe

c.30,000 BC BOW AND ARROW
The bow enabled early hunters to kill animals that stayed beyond the range of their spears. It also helped them to hunt ferocious beasts without danger. The Sahara Desert has now engulfed the North African grasslands where these first archers hunted, but cave paintings prove their early existence.

Cave painting from the Sahara Desert region showing people using bows and arrows

c.25,000 BC THROWING STICK
The traditional weapon of some Aboriginal Australian peoples is the returning boomerang, but this is really a refined throwing stick. Non-returning throwing sticks were probably in use on every continent as early as 25,000 BC. The oldest known example, made from mammoth tusk, comes from what is now Poland.

WORLD EVENTS

600,000–50,001 BC	50,000–20,001 BC

•250,000 BC. The human race has evolved into *Homo sapiens neanderthalensis*. These Neanderthal people are skilled tool makers and are probably religious: they bury their dead and care for the sick. In the 19th century, their fossils will be found in Germany, but the race probably extends far into Asia.

•75,000 BC Hunters develop new weapons and become skilled enough to kill large mammals such as mammoths.

Spear-throwing hunters kill a mammoth

•50,000 BC The last Ice Age is at its peak. Glaciers cover much of northern Europe, locking up water so that the sea is at a very low level.
•42,000 BC The first humans appear in Australia, colonizing the continent from mainland Asia. Though sea levels are low, they still have to travel much of the way over the ocean.

Food wrapped in leaves

•42,000 BC "Modern" human beings, or *Homo sapiens*, possibly spread out from southern Africa; or else the human race evolves simultaneously into the modern form.
•25,000 BC People learn more sophisticated cooking skills, such as wrapping food in leaves to prevent flames from burning it.

20,000 BC

10,000 BC

20,000 BC	18,000 BC	16,000 BC	14,000 BC	12,000 BC	10,000 BC	9000 BC	8000 BC	7000 BC	6000 BC

Iron pyrites

Flint

Percussion fire-making stones

Antler combs

c.12,000 BC
PERCUSSION FIRE-MAKING
By striking the right stones together – a process known as percussion – people discovered that they could create sparks, which in turn would ignite dry shreds of wood. This meant they no longer had to use burning branches from a lightning-struck tree to ignite their fires. They could start a fire whenever they needed one.

c.8000 BC
COMB
The discovery in Scandinavia of antler combs dating from 10,000 years ago might suggest that prehistoric people were well groomed. The reverse is more likely since an important early function of the comb was to remove lice and fleas from hair. Combing was also a useful way to pull hair from hides.

c.18,000 BC BRUSH
The very first painters used their fingers to apply colour to the walls of their rock shelters, but the paintings at Altamira in Spain have lines finer than a fingertip. The artists probably created simple brushes by chewing the end of a fibrous stick, or by shredding fine feathers and tying them to a coarse quill.

Mud brick

c.6000 BC
BRICK
As early people began to settle, they started to build more permanent homes. The first bricks were made of mud and roughly shaped by hand. The hot sun hardened the clay. The first fired bricks appeared in Mesopotamia around 3000 BC.

c.20,000 BC
NEEDLE
As people gradually moved into colder regions, they needed something warmer to wear than simple loincloths and draped fur cloaks. Long thorns may have provided makeshift pins for holding garments together, but by about 20,000 BC, tailors were at work sewing hides together. They used bone needles to pierce the animal skins and joined them with fine strips of sinew or leather thongs.

Bone points (used as needles)

c.10,000 BC
NET
People living near the Mediterranean may have used simple nets for fishing as long ago as 10,000 BC. Their nets would have been very simply made using twisted vines.

c.10,000 BC
STONE HAMMER
The earliest hammers were conveniently sized rocks, used to chip and splinter other stones into useful shapes. By about 10,000 BC, stone workers had added a handle. By 3000 BC, it was a really effective, carefully shaped tool.

c.7000 BC
METAL WORKING
Where copper occurred naturally in high purity, early tool makers just hammered the metal into implements. The hammering hardened the copper so that a simple copper knife remained sharp. The oldest beaten, or cold-worked, copper objects come from Turkey.

c.7000 BC
SPINNING ON A DISTAFF
The first spinners simply twisted threads together in their hands. This laborious technique continued until spinning on a spindle or distaff began some 2,000 years later. The spinner wrapped fibres of wool on the shaft of the spindle, then by turning the spindle, coiled them into a thread.

Harpoon, c.8000 BC   *Twine binding*

Antler spear has a series of barbs. This harpoon was probably used for spearing fish.

Spindle or distaff

Threads are wound around the shaft of the spindle as it turns

c.13,000 BC
HARPOON
As hunters became more skilled, they developed better weapons and more efficient ways to kill their prey. By about 13,000 BC they had invented a harpoon: a spear with a barb, or backwards-pointing spike, at the tip. The barb ensured that the harpoon stayed in the animal's body. The earliest remaining harpoons, made of reindeer antler, come from France. They were made some time between 15,000 and 9500 BC.

c.7500 BC
BOAT
Sea-faring craft probably originated in the eastern Mediterranean around 8000–7000 BC to judge from trade goods there that could only have arrived by sea. Some early evidence of boats comes from Star Carr in Yorkshire, England. Archaeologists found a paddle or rudder which would probably have been used to propel or guide a river-borne canoe. Unfortunately, there was no trace of the craft itself.

Stone weight keeps the distaff turning for longer

20,000–10,001 BC		10,000–5001 BC	

• **18,000 BC** In what will later become Russia, people build houses from huge piles of mammoth bones, stretching skins over the framework to keep out the weather.

• **13,750 BC** In northern Europe, hunters start to capture and tame reindeer, so that they have a readily available source of meat.

Mammoth-bone house

• **13,500–10,000 BC** The last Ice Age ends. Glaciers melt in the northern hemisphere causing worldwide flooding as the sea level rises.

• **12,000 BC** People first domesticate dogs around this time, probably to help them with hunting.

• **10,000 BC** Sabre-toothed tigers become extinct as the large, slow mammals on which their prey become rarer. The tigers' giant canine teeth prevent them from biting effectively, so they cannot live on a diet of smaller mammals.

• **7000 BC** Chickens are domesticated in Southeast Asia.

• **7000 BC** The first rectangular houses are built in the Jordan River Valley. Permanent dwellings were built 2,000 years earlier as farming allowed people to live longer in one place, but these were circular in shape.

• **6800 BC** People begin to tame the goat, keeping it for its skin, milk, and meat.

5000 BC   4375 BC

5000 BC	4875 BC	4750 BC	4625 BC	4500 BC	4375 BC	4250 BC	4125 BC	4000 BC	3875 BC

COUNTING & COMMUNICATION

Einkorn was an early species of wheat.

To prepare wheat for eating, early people ground the grains between two stones (grindstones). The constant rubbing wore the lower stone into a saddle shape.

Table of accounts set out in cuneiform writing

4000–3000 BC WRITING *Sumer*

The earliest known form of writing comes from Sumer. It is called cuneiform (from Latin meaning wedge-shaped) writing. The writer used a wedge-shaped reed to press marks into soft clay tablets. This Sumerian form of writing spread to neighbouring lands where scribes developed it until each character represented not a word, but a sound; combinations of characters created whole words.

Cuneiform on a clay tablet, c.3400 BC

DAILY LIFE & HEALTH

Egyptian grindstones

c.5000 BC GRINDSTONE
Egypt, Mesopotamia
Before agriculture began, cooks pounded the wild seeds they collected to remove the indigestible parts. This left them with a crude form of flour with which to make flat bread. Once people in northern Africa and the eastern Mediterranean region began to cultivate crops such as barley and wheat, they looked for more efficient ways of preparing the larger amounts of grain they had harvested. This is how grinding – rubbing the grain between two stones called grindstones – began.

Einkorn

c.4000 BC PIN *Egypt*
Nature supplies pins in the form of sharp thorns and fish bones, but the first hand-made pins were copper. Egyptian people used stronger bronze to make round-headed pins like these. The first known use of pins was to hold robes together.
See **PIN-MAKING MACHINE AD 1824.**

Bronze "sunflower pins"

AGRICULTURE & INDUSTRY

Ropes supported the mast.

c.5000 BC IRRIGATION *Sumer*
Farmers on the banks of the rivers Tigris, Euphrates, and Nile in the eastern Mediterranean area watched their plants wilt in dust-dry earth. Yet they were within sight of abundant water. To irrigate (water) their fields, they dug ditches which diverted the water towards their crops.

Model of an Egyptian sailing vessel from c.1300 BC

4000–3000 BC ARCH *Indus Valley, Egypt, Mesopotamia*
An arch can bridge wide gaps using only stones or bricks. Small arches were first built in Egypt, the Indus Valley, and Mesopotamia. The Romans improved this building skill and constructed vast arches some 2,000 years later.

CONQUEST

Square sails catch the wind and propel the vessel forward.

4000–3000 BC SAILING VESSELS
Egypt, Mesopotamia
Some time before 3000 BC, the peoples of the eastern Mediterranean region began to add sails to their vessels. Evidence of this comes from an early clay model that was unearthed at Eridu in Mesopotamia: it had a socket for a mast and holes for ropes.

TRAVEL &

Oars for steering

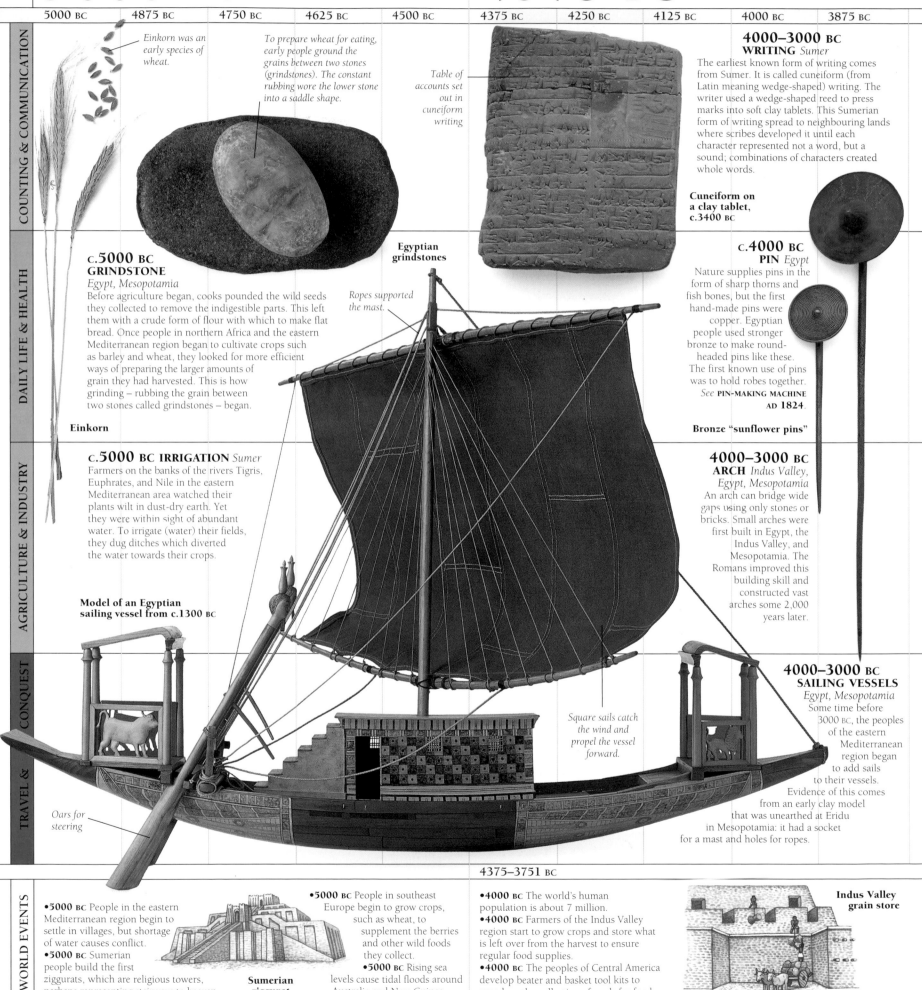

WORLD EVENTS

4375–3751 BC

- **5000 BC** People in the eastern Mediterranean region begin to settle in villages, but shortage of water causes conflict.
- **5000 BC** Sumerian people build the first ziggurats, which are religious towers, perhaps representing stairways to heaven.

Sumerian ziggurat

- **5000 BC** People in southeast Europe begin to grow crops, such as wheat, to supplement the berries and other wild foods they collect.
- **5000 BC** Rising sea levels cause tidal floods around Australia and New Guinea.

- **4000 BC** The world's human population is about 7 million.
- **4000 BC** Farmers of the Indus Valley region start to grow crops and store what is left over from the harvest to ensure regular food supplies.
- **4000 BC** The peoples of Central America develop beater and basket tool kits to speed up the collection of seeds for food.

Indus Valley grain store

3750 BC
3125 BC

Case is made of a rare form of rock called anhydrite

Container for black eye paint

Applicators have flattened ends for putting on eye paint.

Egyptian cosmetics containers and applicators

c.3700 BC COSMETICS *Egypt*
Many ancient peoples painted their skin. Egyptian men and women wore make-up, not only for vanity, but also to reduce the glare of the sun and the irritation of their eyes. They painted their eyes with a mixture of soot, black lead, and antimony.

3500–3000 BC MIRROR *Egypt*
Metal mirrors were a great luxury for nearly 5,000 years because of the difficulty in making a perfectly flat, highly polished metal surface.

c.3500 BC NAIL *Mesopotamia*
The first copper nails were soft and costly, so most ancient furniture had to be made with carved joints.

Bronze surface would have been polished and reflective when new

Egyptian hand mirror

c.3200 BC INK *Egypt*
The invention of papyrus (reed paper) in 3500 BC forced Egyptian scribes to mix pigments that would not flake off their flexible documents, so they made the first inks. They used natural gum from the bark of an acacia tree and mixed it with soot.

Glass beads

c.2600 BC SET-SQUARE *Egypt*
Ancient Egyptian architects knew that they could make a perfect right angle using a triangular set-square. It had sides in the proportion 3:4:5. With this knowledge, they were able to set out walls of buildings very precisely. They could measure corners and check that surfaces were level.

Egyptian bronze set-square

3000–2500 BC GLASS *Egypt, Mesopotamia*
The first glass objects were possibly created to imitate gems, but complex early glass-making technology may have made them as costly as the real thing. Egyptian glass workers made simple glass beads as early as 3000 BC. *See* GLASS BOTTLE 1500 BC *and* GLASS BLOWING 100 BC.

c.3000 BC HARP *Mesopotamia*
The harp is the earliest known stringed instrument and may have been developed from the bow. As it was shaped like a bow, it could probably only play low notes; the frame was not strong enough to withstand the string tension required for a higher pitch. The number of strings on a harp was chosen for symbolic as well as musical reasons: some believed that five-stringed harps prevented suffering.

Egyptian five-stringed harp

Early bronze sword

c.3500 BC BRONZE *Mesopotamia*
Pure copper is too soft for tools. Only with the invention of bronze – an alloy (mixture) of copper and tin – did metal tools begin to replace those of stone. Weapons, too, took a great leap forward with its discovery. A bronze sword was sharper and lighter than any flint axe. A warrior with bronze weapons therefore had an enormous advantage over a Stone-Age opponent.

c.3500 BC PLOUGH *Mesopotamia*
Early Sumerian farmers of Mesopotamia broke up the ground with a simple digging stick or hoe. Weighting the hoe made it more effective and attaching handles enabled the farmer to drag it along. By tying the plough to the horns of an ox, farmers took much of the hard work out of tilling fields.

Barbed fish hooks

Barb
Hook

c.3000 BC PLUMB LINE *Egypt*
Egyptian builders were the first to use a plumb line – a weighted cord. They knew that their constructions stood exactly upright when they were parallel with the line.

c.3000 BC BARBED FISH HOOK *Scandinavia*
A barbed fish hook increased the size of a day's catch by stopping fish from taking the bait and swimming away with it.

Roman plumb line

c.2800 BC HEMP ROPE *China*
Hemp fibre was first used for making rope in China. It was much stronger than the rope that the Egyptians had made from reeds and date-palm fibres. Hemp rope eventually replaced all other types of rope and was in use until the invention of synthetic fibres in the 20th century.

Common hemp

c.3200 BC WHEEL *Mesopotamia*
Three centuries after the invention of the potter's wheel in Mesopotamia, simple vehicle wheels appeared in the same area. The first wheels were crude and solid, made from three planks. These were pegged together, and cut to a circular shape. The planks turned on a fixed axle.

Reconstruction of a plank wheel

c.3000 BC YOKE *Mesopotamia*
Early farmers of Mesopotamia realized that the broad backs of the animals they were herding could carry quite heavy loads over long distances. The yoke (a wooden frame) rested across the shoulders of a pair of oxen, enabling them to drag a heavily laden sled or to pull a plough more effectively.

Cord has rotted: this is a modern replacement

Fibrous stems were used for rope making

Bronze plumb bob keeps line vertical

•**3550 BC** Chinese farmers use simple methods of farming, moving to new fields when they have exhausted the soil.
•**3500 BC** The Sumerian civilization reaches its height.
•**3500 BC** Cultivation of crop plants, and herding of animals has spread through Europe from the Mediterranean as far north as Scandinavia.
•**3400 BC** In Egypt, the Pharaoh Menes unites and rules the Northern and Southern Kingdoms.
•**3200 BC** Small settlements in the Indus Valley have already grown into large villages. In 500 years' time, these become the world's first cities.

Pharaoh Menes in conquest

•**3000 BC** The world's population reaches about 14 million.
•**3000 BC** Overgrazing and bad farming methods in northern Africa begin to turn the soil to desert.
•**3000 BC** Farmers in the Andes Mountains of South America start to grow potatoes.
•**2900 BC** In Egypt, slaves begin building the Great Pyramid of Cheops at Giza.
•**2700 BC** Chinese Emperor Shen Nung develops the principles of herbal medicine, and acupuncture is used to relieve toothache.
•**2600 BC** Egyptian people start to sun-dry food to preserve it.

2500 BC

2125 BC

2500 BC	2425 BC	2350 BC	2275 BC	2200 BC	2125 BC	2050 BC	1975 BC	1900 BC	1825 BC

COUNTING & COMMUNICATION

**c.2500 BC
STANDARD WEIGHTS** *Mesopotamia*
People used to measure weight by using natural produce, such as grain, for comparison. They soon realized that the weight of foods can vary so standardized systems of weights were invented. The first of these began in Sumer and was surprisingly accurate. Early weights from the region were made of stone and carved into the shape of sleeping geese.

Stone goose weight, Mesopotamia

Hand-painted clay balls

c.1950 BC STANDARD RULER *Mesopotamia*
The first known standard measure of length was a heavy copper bar, unearthed at Nippur on the River Euphrates. It is marked with four large units, each divided into 16 smaller units, much like imperial feet and inches.

An Egyptian game of "catch"

DAILY LIFE & HEALTH

**c.2500 BC
BATHS** *Indus Valley*
The earliest bath is perhaps a square tub found in Gaza dating from 3100 BC (this may have been a storage tank). By 2500 BC, many houses in the Indus Valley had baths and elaborate drains.

c.2350 BC LAVATORY *Mesopotamia*
The first lavatories were built into the Akkadian palace at Eshnunna, Mesopotamia. They were simple pedestals, sometimes with a shaped seat of bitumen (tar). No water sealed them from the sewer that ran beneath, so smells and flies were probably a problem in summer.

**c.2000 BC
BALL** *Egypt, Lydia*
Balls were probably the earliest children's toys. The first reliable records of ball games we have are from Egyptian tomb paintings from around 2000 BC.

**c.1800 BC
MEDICAL INSTRUMENTS** *Babylon*
Early evidence of the use of medical instruments comes from the Babylonian code of Hammurabi. It contains a scale of fees and punishments for surgeons, for example: "If the doctor shall open an abscess with a bronze knife and kill the patient… his hand shall be cut off."

Mummified Egyptian woman

Head support

c.2300 BC EMBALMING *Egypt*
Belief in life after death led early people to try to embalm dead bodies to prevent them from rotting. The Egyptians were the first to have any success: they started protecting their dead with resin and a coating of plaster, later perfecting the process to mummification.

Roman medical instruments, AD 100–300

Folding knife

Probe to explore wounds

AGRICULTURE & INDUSTRY

Decorative wax plate to cover embalming incision

The mummy was put inside its tomb and packed in layers of linen to protect it.

Embalming incision where organs were removed

Remains of linen bandages

Iron reaping hook

Iron blade

**c.1900 BC
IRON SMELTING** *Mesopotamia*
Ancient people called the iron that fell from meteorites "metal from heaven". However, when Mesopotamian metal workers began iron smelting (extracting a metal from an ore using heat), they began to view iron less favourably. Iron ore required more fuel for smelting than the copper used to make bronze: it was hard to mould and rusted easily. Iron work did not expand until about 1200 BC when people learned to make steel by decreasing the carbon content.

Double-ended traction hook

Grab-rail for charioteer

TRAVEL & CONQUEST

Flint-bladed knife to make incision

Toe- and fingernails still preserved

Antler horn handle

**c.2180 BC
TUNNEL** *Babylon*
The history of tunnel-making is difficult to trace. A tunnel that passed beneath the River Euphrates is said to have been built in around 2180 BC. However, we have no firm proof of its existence. The oldest remaining tunnel lies on the Greek island of Samos in the Aegean Sea. It was built in 687 BC and was about 1,000 m (1,100 yd) long.

**c.2000 BC
CHARIOT** *Mesopotamia*
The combination of horse, harness, bridle, and a lightweight two-wheeled cart gave the Mesopotamians a powerful war machine. Horse-drawn chariots could travel much faster than foot soldiers, who often panicked and ran away from this terrifying sight.

Spoked wheels – invented around 2000 BC – were much lighter than earlier plank wheels.

Chariots were small and lightweight for maximum speed.

WORLD EVENTS

2500–2126 BC

- **2300 BC** Rise of the Indus Valley civilization in India and Pakistan.
- **2500 BC** Central and northern European peoples are still using stone tools, long after bronze tools have replaced them in the eastern Mediterranean region.
- **2500 BC** In Peru, cotton is cultivated for making fabric.

Babylonian map

- **2500 BC** Beaker people (so called because of their distinctive pottery) travel across northern Europe and reach Britain.
- **2500 BC** People of Central Asia start to tame horses.
- **2300 BC** The earliest surviving "world map" is carved on a piece of baked clay from Babylon.

2125–1751 BC

- **2000 BC** The world's human population is about 27 million.
- **2000 BC** Mayan people move inland from the coasts of Mexico. They plant maize and worship a maize god.
- **2000–1450 BC** Minoans build large palaces on Crete, including the Palace of Minos at Knossos,

Hammurabi's laws

legendary home of the Minotaur monster – half man, half beast.
- **1900 BC** An earthquake destroys the cities of Sodom and Gomorrah on the Dead Sea – now part of Israel.
- **1800–1750 BC** In Mesopotamia, King Hammurabi introduces the first written laws, covering family, civil, criminal, and commercial offences.

1750 BC

1750 BC	1675 BC	1600 BC

c.1700 BC ALPHABET *Phoenicia*

The first written characters represented simple sounds, rather than whole words. Several civilizations developed their own methods of writing, but the Phoenician people produced the first true alphabet containing 22 letters. From this Phoenician version, the Greek alphabet grew; this in turn developed into the Latin letters used in many parts of the world today.

Early Phoenician pottery

The Phoenician inscription on this piece of broken pottery is the name of a goddess.

Adding copper or cobalt salts to glass produced a rich blue.

Yellow glass was made with antimony compounds.

Phoenician glass vessel

c.1500 BC GLASS BOTTLE

Egypt, Greece, Phoenicia

Decorative glass first appeared in about 3000 BC, but it wasn't until around 1500 BC that glass workers learned to make vessels. They dipped a sand-filled cloth bag into a vat of melted glass, which coated the bag and took its shape. The sand was emptied out and the bag disintegrated, leaving a glass bottle. *See* **GLASS 3000 BC** *and* **GLASS BLOWING 100 BC.**

c.1500 BC WOODEN SPOON *Various*

The first spoons were probably simple shells. For thousands of years the spoon was largely a cook's tool, but ancient Greeks used spoons exclusively for eating eggs.

Wooden spoons like this ancient Egyptian one were in common use in many parts of the world by 1500 BC, but most have rotted away with time.

Early Roman bronze model of a horse and chariot

Figure with sling from a Syrian relief, 9th century BC

1375 BC

1375 BC	1300 BC	1225 BC

c.1200 BC BELLS *China*

During the Shang dynasty (1600–1027 BC), Chinese people developed sophisticated bronze-casting technology, and with their skills they created the first bells. Bell casting in the rest of the world did not reach the same level of perfection until the 8th or 9th centuries AD.

Chinese bell, Zhou dynasty (1122–221 BC)

This bell was once part of a group of chimes that hung from a frame.

c.1350 BC SHOWER

Egypt, Greece

Purpose-built showers can be traced back to 1350 BC. At Akhenaten, the ancient capital of Egypt, archaeologists identified a shallow slab, which some believed to be a shower pan. A Greek vase painting (*right*) from the 6th century BC shows women showering under what appear to be specially made shower heads.

c.1350 BC WELDING *Syria*

To weld together two pieces of iron, a metal worker must heat them to a very high temperature and hammer them together. The first example of welding was a head-rest found in the tomb of Egyptian King Tutankhamun. It was perhaps a gift from a Syrian king. (Egyptian iron working was not very skilled at that time.)

c.1200 BC ENAMEL *Cyprus*

The art of decorating a metal surface with coloured glass was known in the ancient empires of Egypt and Mesopotamia. However, the first true enamel work was made by the Mycenaeans in Cyprus. Rings found in a tomb at Old Paphos have tiny wire cells called cloisons set in the enamel. These separate the different colours of glaze.

To fire a stone from a sling, a soldier would hold the two ends of string, whirl it around his head, then release one end of the string, propelling the shot forward.

1400–1200 BC SLING *Obscure*

Archaeologists have found shaped stones and clay pellets that Stone-Age people may have fired from slings or slingshots as long ago as 4500 BC. The slings themselves have never been found, but slings have not changed in style since earliest times. They were clearly in use by about 1200 BC, since the Bible refers to an army of crack-shots: "Among all these people there were seven hundred chosen men left-handed; every one could sling stones at an hair-breadth, and not miss." (Judges 20: 16).

Inca sling, Peru, 15th century AD

Braided wool cradle for stone ammunition

1750–1376 BC	

•**1750 BC** Indus Valley culture collapses. Excessive irrigation has made soils too salty for agriculture.
•**1700 BC** Abraham, from the Mesopotamian city of Ur, establishes the religion of Judaism.
•**1600 BC** In England, the building of Stonehenge – a circle of huge stones – is completed.

•**1600 BC** Greek foot soldiers start to wear body armour in battle.
•**1500 BC** Cattle and goats are first domesticated in Africa.
•**1500 BC** Chinese weavers begin to make silk fabric, establishing a craft that will soon link the Eastern and Western worlds through trade.
•**1500–600 BC** Hindu religion grows.

1375–1001 BC	

•**1361 BC** Nine-year-old Tutankhamun becomes Pharaoh (king) of Egypt.
•**1340 BC** Tutankhamun is buried in the Valley of the Kings, Egypt.
•**1200 BC** Following persecution in Egypt, the Hebrews return to Canaan.
•**1200–1000 BC** The Phoenicians rise to power in the Mediterranean.

Tutankhamun

Their cities, Tyre and Sidon, are famous for purple dye, glass, and metal goods.
•**1190 BC** After a siege lasting 10 years, the city of Troy falls to Greek warriors, who enter the city by hiding in a huge wooden horse.

Trojan Horse

1000 BC

| 1000 BC | 950 BC | 900 BC | 850 BC | 800 BC | 750 BC | | 600 BC | 550 BC |

COUNTING & COMMUNICATION

1000–700 BC SUNDIAL *Egypt*

The earliest methods of measuring time took advantage of the Sun's steady movement across the sky. The first shadow clocks we know of were Egyptian: they were posts hammered into the ground. The length of the shadow indicated the time. Such simple clocks were very imprecise, but by about 700 BC the sundial had developed into something resembling its modern form. A tilted gnomon (the arm on a sundial) cast a shadow that stayed the same length throughout the day, and the shadow's angle, not its length, indicated the time on a circular scale.

Crossed sticks set at right angles to one another

Stone weights

Replica of an ancient Egyptian groma

600–300 BC SURVEYING INSTRUMENTS *Egypt*

Egyptian surveyors could check that walls and fences were straight by viewing them through the merkhet, or slit palm leaf. They also invented the groma to set out squares and rectangles. This was a simple cross of wood held horizontally. Plumb lines hanging from each stick allowed surveyors to sight along lines at exact right angles. *See* **PLUMB LINE 3000 BC.**

Serrated blade

DAILY LIFE & HEALTH

Handle for pushing and pulling saw through wood

Iron saw

800–700 BC IRON SAW *Assyria*

The earliest saws were simple notched flint blades and they were probably little better than scrapers. Only with the smelting of metals did the saw become a useful cutting tool. The Assyrians were using iron frame saws in Mesopotamia between 800 and 700 BC.

c.700 BC FALSE TEETH *Etruria, Italy*

The Etruscan people who lived in central Italy were the first to eat with false teeth. Etruscan dentists used gold straps to fit animals' teeth into their wealthy clients' gaps. Poor Etruscans could not afford false teeth; they cured their toothache with a mouthwash made by boiling dogs' teeth in wine.

Etruscan dentures

c.620 BC COINS
Lydia, Asia Minor

The first traders bartered (swapped) goods, but this was inconvenient when they started to travel greater distances. Loose gold had to be weighed out so it was easier to carry coins of standard weight instead. They were made from electrum, a mixture of gold and silver.

Lydian coins

AGRICULTURE & INDUSTRY

c.1000 BC SUGAR REFINING *India*

A few vague references in ancient Indian texts suggest that Indian farmers were growing sugar cane and refining its sap as early as 1000 BC. The first taste that European tongues had of the sweetness of this gigantic grass was in 325 BC – the year King Alexander the Great invaded India with his army. His men were impressed by the way the Indians were able to make syrup as sweet as honey without bees and wanted to learn how it was done.

Sugar cane crops as shown on an Assyrian relief

Two pieces of ox-bone filed to size and riveted to a gold band.

c.600 BC WINCH, WINDLASS *Obscure*

The remains of a winch dating from 600 BC have been found in Austria. The main purpose of a winch, or windlass, was to give labourers more lifting power when hauling on a rope. It was thus an essential part of the crane. More unusually, the Greek doctor Hippocrates is said to have used one for stretching limbs!

Aqueduct

Water flows across the top

A series of arches support the structure and the weight of the water.

TRAVEL & CONQUEST

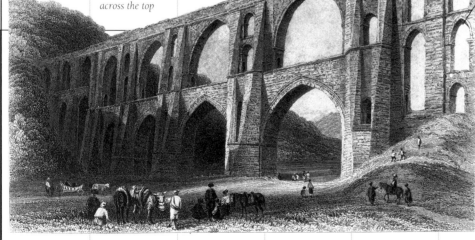

c.690 BC AQUEDUCT *Assyria*

Where ancient canals passed over a valley, the builders constructed an aqueduct (left) to bridge the dip. The first large aqueduct was built as part of an ambitious Assyrian water system. A 9-m (30-ft) span arch carried an 18.3 m (20-yd) wide canal across a 274-m (300-yd) valley on its way to the capital, Nineveh. There the canal watered the gardens of King Sennacherib.

Ptolemaic map

550–510 BC MAP *Greece*

Landowners drew plans of their estates more than 4,000 years ago, but the ancient Greeks were the first to draw travellers' maps of large areas. The maps that Hecataeus, Anaximander, and other Greeks drew in the 6th century BC remained the best available until the 2nd century AD when Claudius Ptolemy improved on them. We only know of his maps from 15th-century copies (above).

WORLD EVENTS

| 1000–751 BC | 750–501 BC |

- **1000 BC** In North America the mound builders construct burial mounds and other earthworks.
- **1000 BC** People in China cut ice from frozen lakes in winter, and store it to chill food in summer.
- **973 BC** In Israel, King Solomon orders the building of the temple at Jerusalem.

Etruscan decoration

- **900 BC** The Etruscans start to establish towns in central Italy.
- **800–700 BC** Homer writes the *Odyssey*, about an epic sea voyage.
- **776 BC** The first Olympic Games take place in Greece. The only race is a foot race of 183 m (200 yd). Women are not allowed to compete.
- **753 BC** The city of Rome is founded.

- **671 BC** Egypt is conquered by the Assyrians.
- **612 BC** The Assyrian Empire collapses when the Assyrians are defeated by the Babylonians and Medes.
- **605–562 BC** The Hanging Gardens of Babylon are built for King Nebuchadnezzar.

Buddha

- **550 BC** Pythagoras develops his mathematical theorem, which explains the size relationship of the sides of a right-angled triangle.
- **528 BC** In India, Siddhartha Gautama (Buddha, or "enlightened one") establishes the religion of Buddhism.
- **509 BC** Rome becomes a republic.

500 BC

250 BC

c.450 BC ABACUS
Mediterranean countries
The origins of this first calculating device are hard to trace. The very first abacus was probably a dust-covered tray on which the clerk counted in fingermarks. This method of calculation was in use at least 2,450 years ago in the Mediterranean area. The more modern form of abacus, with beads on rods, is a Chinese invention from about AD 200.

c.300 BC
WATER CLOCK *Egypt*
Water clocks were in use in Alexandria, Egypt in 1400 BC, but were little better than graduated leaking buckets. Greek inventor Ctesibius of Alexandria created a much more precise water clock. His geared device, called a clepsydra, measured time in Egyptian hours, which changed in length according to the season.

Engraving of Ctesibius' water clock

c.190 BC
PARCHMENT *Asia Minor*
People in the ancient city of Pergamum began to make a new writing surface from animal skin called parchment. The untanned skin was scraped, cleaned with lime to remove fat, and then stretched on a frame and left to dry. Parchment did not decay as quickly as papyrus – an Egyptian writing material made of the reed-like papyrus plant.

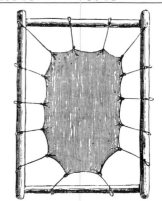

c.500 BC CARPET *China*
Floor-coverings were made of reeds long before knotted carpets appeared. The first knotted carpets were probably the products of Chinese or Persian workshops and were found in the Altai Mountains on the border between China and Mongolia.

c.300 BC
MUSICAL ORGAN
Alexandria, Egypt
Ctesibius worked out that he could use pressure from another of his inventions – the piston pump – to power a simple organ. Water from the pump flowed into a sealed chamber, forcing air out through a series of tuned pipes. Keys controlled the air flow, so that a musician could pick out a tune.

Roman mosaic showing an early musical organ

Model of Archimedes' screw in use

By turning the handle in a circle the screw revolves.

Screw lifts water upwards

Grain to be milled

Milled flour

Water supply

Millstone

Water wheel

Model of a Greek mill

c.236 BC
ARCHIMEDES' SCREW *Obscure*
Long before pumps came into widespread use, farmers raised water for irrigation with the Archimedian screw. This was an inclined screw-shaped tube. Turning the screw with the lower end submerged lifted water to the top. It is named after Archimedes, the Greek engineer, who wrote about it in 236 BC.

c.85 BC MILL *Greece*
The invention of the water-powered mill meant that people no longer had to grind grain for flour using a mortar and pestle (a bowl and beater). The first simple mill wheels revolved horizontally, and only worked well in fast-flowing streams. They were nonetheless important because they were among the first labour-saving devices.

c.100 BC
GLASS BLOWING *Syria*
Syrian glass makers developed a less costly method of producing glass than hand moulding. They put a blob of glass on the end of a long pipe and then blew through the other end. This formed a bubble that could be shaped and cut to make bottles or open vessels.

Roman blown glass bottle

Early blown glass like this was made in moulds, but glass makers later learned to work the bubbles freely.

This tiny bottle has been blown into a grape-shaped mould.

c.400 BC CATAPULT *Greece*
The huge crossbows that Greek engineers built during the rule of Dionysius (405–367 BC) were really giant catapults because they fired rocks instead of arrows. The forerunners of modern artillery, they had a range of about 300 m (1,000 ft). Devices like this are mentioned in the Bible: they are called "engines, invented by cunning men" (Chronicles II: 26).

Wooden cup to hold missile

Verge or throwing arm

Rope to pull throwing arm back when ready for fire

Replica of a catapult used in 15th century AD

c.480 BC
PONTOON BRIDGE *Persia*
The first recorded pontoon bridge – a bridge with floating supports – was built by the Persians under King Xerxes. Some 676 ships in two rows bridged the Bosphorus – the strait that divides Europe and Asia.

•**490 BC** The Greek army repels a larger Persian force at Marathon; messenger Pheidippides dies of exhaustion after running the 26 miles to Athens to announce the victory. The marathon race is named after his feat.

Marathon runners

•**457 BC** Greek civilization enters a "Golden Age" of art and architecture. Two thirds of Athenians are slaves.
•**307 BC** Ptolemy II establishes a great library at Alexandria, Egypt.
•**285 BC** First known lighthouse is built at Pharos, Egypt.
•**260 BC** Emperor Asoka of India plants herb gardens for medicinal use.

•**250 BC** The Roman spectacle of gladiators is introduced. Slaves fight to the death to entertain crowds.
•**240 BC** The Greek geographer Eratosthenes calculates the size of the Earth. He comes within 10 or 15 per cent of modern measurements.
•**215 BC** The building of the Great Wall of China begins. Centuries later, it is the only artificial structure visible from space.

Great Wall of China

0   200

0	40	80	120	160	200	240	280	320	360

COUNTING & COMMUNICATION

Dividers for drawing circles

•79 DIVIDERS AND CALIPERS *Italy*
Roman masons and carpenters were among the first to draw circles with the aid of dividers or compasses and to transfer measurements using calipers. Archaeologists discovered both of these drawing instruments in the ruins of the ancient Roman city of Pompeii.

Woody plants are chopped and soaked in water.

Mixture is pounded with more water to make pulp.

Fibres are matted together and paper mixture is spread out to dry on mesh.

Chinese paper-making process

•105 PAPER *China*
A Chinese court official, Tsai Lun, is generally given the credit for inventing paper in about AD 105. He discovered that almost any plant fibre would make good paper if it was ground up and soaked in water. The Chinese guarded the secret of paper making jealously and it did not reach Europe for more than a thousand years.

A large barrow is attached to either side of the wheel for carrying heavy loads.

DAILY LIFE & HEALTH

Two pointed ends: one holds the dividers in place while the other is turned to etch a circle

The Pantheon was made of concrete. Roman engineers produced the first concrete around 200 BC by adding volcanic ash to a mixture of quicklime, sand, and gravel.

Concrete used at top of dome is lightweight to reduce load on walls

200–300 WHEELBARROW *China*
The humble wheelbarrow is deceptively simple. By the use of levers and a single wheel, it enables a worker to carry a very heavy load quite long distances. The same load formerly required two workers – one for each end of a stretcher – so the wheelbarrow could easily double the productivity of a building worker. The Chinese called it the wooden ox or gliding horse and sometimes equipped their wheelbarrows with sails.

Tomb rubbing showing a wheelbarrow, China

AGRICULTURE & INDUSTRY

Steam is forced up into pipes

Steam escaping from jets makes ball rotate

Boiling water

Fire

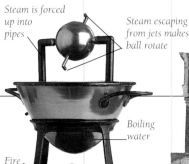
Hero's steam machine

•50 STEAM MACHINE *Greece*
Harnessing the power of steam is an ancient dream. The Greek inventor Hero devised a steam machine – a primitive steam turbine shaped like a globe with a pair of jets. Feeding steam into this sphere made it spin as the steam flowed out through the jets. Hero treated his invention as a novelty rather than a useful source of power.

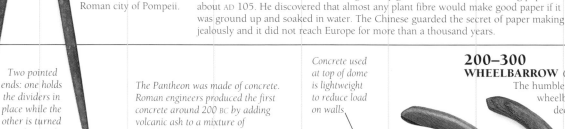

Lower down, heavy basalt rock gave concrete strength

Cutaway model of the Pantheon, Rome

124–128 DOME *Italy*
Domes, like arches, present the builder with special problems because they are not stable until the final stone is in place. Builders of early domes made their constructions pointed at the top and used rings of masonry that were self-supporting. True domes such as the enormous 43.2-m (142-ft) diameter Pantheon in Rome required an internal support during construction. The Pantheon, completed around AD 128, was made possible by the Romans' skill as builders and their expert use of concrete.

Farmer guided mouldboard plough using curved handles

TRAVEL & CONQUEST

25–220 SADDLE *China*
Bareback horse-riding demands considerable skill, and handicaps the rider, who must balance carefully to stay on the horse. The padded saddle, which makes horse-riding more comfortable and easier, was a Chinese invention.

c.50 HORSESHOE *Italy*
In the first century the Romans were developing ways of protecting horses' feet on hard ground. They made hipposandals – tied-on metal horseshoes. At about the same time, nailed-on shoes also appeared. They not only protected the horse's foot, but also provided a better grip.

Hipposandal

•200 SKATES *Scandinavia*
Evidence of skating dates back only to AD 200: an iron skate from about that date has been found in Scandinavia. However, experts believe the earliest skates were probably splinters of bone fixed to boots. (The word "skate" comes from a Dutch word meaning leg or shank bone.) A pole was probably used as a lever to help skaters move forward.

Viking boot and skate, 10th century

The boot was not attached to the bone; the weight of the skater kept it in place.

WORLD EVENTS

0–199

•**1** The population of the world is about 170 million people.
•**61** Boudicca, warrior queen of an English tribe, leads a revolt against Roman rule. Before being defeated, her armies kill thousands of Romans.
•**64** The city of Rome is burnt to the ground.

Queen Boudicca

•**79** Mt. Vesuvius erupts and destroys the city of Pompeii in Italy.
•**100** Teotihuacan in Mexico has grown to a city of 50,000 people.
•**122** The Romans build Hadrian's wall to stop an invasion of England by the Picts in Scotland.
•**125** In northern Africa, a great plague kills 500,000 people.

200–399

•**201** Empress Jingo rules Japan. According to Japanese legend, she has the power to control the tides.
•**200–300** The Hopewell people continue and expand the mound-building tradition started by the Adena culture in America's Mississippi region.
•**320** Under northern India's Gupta dynasty, science and the arts flourish.

Mica hand, Hopewell

•**337** Constantine the Great becomes the first Christian Roman emperor.
•**370** The Huns – Mongols – reach Europe from Asia. Led by Attila, they later conquer large parts of the continent.
•**395** The Roman Empire, which has ruled much of Europe for six centuries, splits into two.

400

400	440	480	520

600

600	640	680	720	760

•500
STENCIL *China, Japan*

Brushing or rubbing ink through shapes, or stencils, cut in a sheet of ink-proof material is a quick and simple way of transferring patterns or words. This method of printing is called stencilling. The stencil shown here follows similar principles. It is an image drawn in ink on flimsy paper, through which a pin could be pricked to transfer the outline of the image neatly on to another surface.

Stencil of a Buddha on a lotus flower, China

Tiny holes so that stencil can be etched out with a pin.

Bone or horn elephant – equivalent of modern bishop

Scandinavian chess pieces, 11th–14th century

Chinese paper money issued in 1287

•600
CHESS *India*

The origins of chess are difficult to trace. The most likely inventors are the Indians, who played a similar game called *chaturanga*. Chess came to Europe via the Arabic nations, and by the 15th century, chess pieces looked much like they do today.

618–906
PAPER MONEY *China*

The sophisticated idea of using bank notes originated in China during the T'ang dynasty (618–906), but paper money was not widely used until Mongol Emperor Kublai Khan began to use it to pay his troops in the 13th century.

Pushing the tail pole turned the sails into the wind

600•
MOULDBOARD PLOUGH *Europe*

The simple plough could work the sandy soils bordering the Mediterranean but it was no match for the heavy clays of northern Europe. So by the 7th century, the German people had developed a heavier, more effective plough. Drawn by a pair of oxen, the mouldboard plough did much to shape the landscape of northern Europe. It even gave shape to two basic units of measure: a furlong is the length of one ploughed strip, at the end of which the oxen rested; and an acre is the area a team could plough in a day.

Mouldboard to turn clods of earth over and bury weeds

Mouldboard plough

The coulter – a vertical knife to cut turf

Early mouldboards were made of a smooth wood such as apple, or beech. Metal mouldboards like this eventually replaced wood which soon wore out.

•635 QUILL PEN *Spain*

St. Isidore of Seville, writing in the 7th century, was the first to refer to a pen made from a goose quill, although they may have been in use earlier. Feathers for quills were buried in hot sand to remove unwanted membrane, then hardened in acid and sharpened.

Scribes had to sharpen the nib constantly as it quickly wore down.

c.740
WOOD BLOCK PRINTING *Japan, China*

Printing from carved wooden blocks was first used in Asia to print copies of prayer sheets or charms.

•683 ZERO *Cambodia, Indonesia*

In an Arabic (modern) number, each digit multiplies a factor of ten (such as 10, 100, 1000) and the digit's position shows which factor to multiply. When one position is empty, we write a zero as a "placeholder". Zero was a revolutionary breakthrough when it first appeared in Asia. Arab mathematician Muhammad ibn Al-khwarizmi took it to Europe in the 8th century.

Persian mill sails turned on a vertical axis; the sails of later European mills like this one turned on a shaft that was almost horizontal.

Brake wheel

Millstones contained in here

Model of a European post mill

•650 WINDMILL *Persia*

The first reports of windmills came from Persia. The sails of these early mills turned on a vertical shaft, which drove the millstones directly. European post mills, which had sails turning on a horizontal shaft, appeared in Portugal five centuries later. In some areas, windmills became more popular than water mills for grinding flour.

•674
NAPALM *Syria*

According to legend, its inventor was Kallenikos, an architect from Syria. By squirting the "sea-fire" from bronze tubes, the Byzantium navy set fire to the Arab fleet in 674. When dropped from aircraft, modern napalm is like burning syrup which sticks to its victims.

c.400 Alchemy begins in Europe. Alchemists' aims – to cure all ills, and change lead to gold – are impossible, but they lay one of the foundation stones of modern science.
•**432** St. Patrick converts the Irish to Christianity.
•**449** Jutes, Angles, and Saxons from the area that is now Denmark begin to conquer parts of Britain, driving the Celtic people west to Wales.
•**450** In the Pacific, chief Hawaii-Loa sails across 2,400 miles of ocean to discover the Hawaiian Islands.
•**450** The Basket Maker III period of the Anasazi culture starts in southwest America. Pottery-making technology grows in importance.

St. Patrick

•**610** In a cave close to Mecca, the prophet Mohammed has a vision calling on him to preach the message of God. His teachings establish the Islamic religion.
•**711** Moorish people (Arabs and Berbers) move into southern Europe. They rule parts of the region until the 17th century.

Viking ship

•**768** On the death of their father, Charlemagne and his brother inherit a kingdom covering France and part of Germany. Charlemagne soon builds a vast Christian empire in Europe.
•**789** Viking people from the Scandinavian region make raids on the English east coast.

800   925

800	825	850	875	900	925	950	975	1000	1025

COUNTING & COMMUNICATION

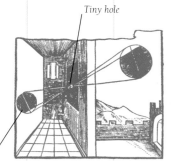

Frontispiece to the *Diamond Sutra* – the world's earliest printed book

c.868
BOOK PRINTING *China*
Chinese scholars were pioneers of book printing. The oldest known printed book is in scroll form and is called the *Diamond Sutra*. The book was printed in AD 868 using carved wooden blocks. Engraving each block was a time-consuming way to create letters, yet Chinese printers went on to print the Buddhist holy book, the *Tripitaka*. This required more than 130,000 carved blocks, and the task was completed in AD 983.

These blocks were used in the same way as Chinese moveable type.

Early Turkish type blocks

c.1040
MOVEABLE TYPE PRINTING *China*
Chinese alchemist Pi Cheng used baked clay to produce the first known moveable type around 1040. After printing, he separated and re-used the type. Wang Chen improved this system by using wooden letters around 1300 and used them to publish a book. The idea of moveable type reached Europe much later. In 1438, Johannes Gutenberg began to print from moulded metal letters in Mainz, Germany.
See **PRINTING PRESS 1450**.

DAILY LIFE & HEALTH

c.840
CAMERA OBSCURA *China*
Today's cameras trace their history to the camera obscura, or darkened room. A pinhole in the room's window shutters allowed an image of a sunlit landscape outside to be projected on to the facing wall, without the aid of a lens.

Tiny hole

Image of solar eclipse

Camera obscura projecting a solar eclipse on to a wall

Wooden wheel

Bobbin with yarn wound on to it

European spinning wheel, the Great Wheel

c.1000
SPINNING WHEEL *Asia*
Around the start of the 11th century, textile workers in India first used the wheel to help spin yarn. Meanwhile, improvements to the Chinese silk-reeling machine made it resemble a modern spinning wheel. By the end of the century, the process was complete and the Chinese wheel twisted the threads together before reeling them. The spinning wheel was unknown in Europe until the early 14th century. Its arrival greatly increased the output of yarn.

AGRICULTURE & INDUSTRY

Padded horse collar

c.900
HORSE COLLAR AND HARNESS *Europe*
In a simple harness, a horse could pull about 60 kg (135 lb); heavier loads forced the harness on to the horse's windpipe. The invention of the padded horse collar greatly increased the load-carrying capacity of the horse and made pulling a plough a lot easier.

A rounded cam operating a piston pump

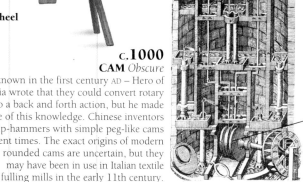

Cam

c.1000
CAM *Obscure*
Cams were known in the first century AD – Hero of Alexandria wrote that they could convert rotary movement to a back and forth action, but he made little use of this knowledge. Chinese inventors operated trip-hammers with simple peg-like cams from ancient times. The exact origins of modern rounded cams are uncertain, but they may have been in use in Italian textile fulling mills in the early 11th century.

TRAVEL & CONQUEST

Chinese experiments with gunpowder

c.950 GUNPOWDER *China*
Explosives revolutionized warfare in Europe, but the vital ingredient for all firearms – gunpowder – was a 10th-century Chinese invention. Early gunpowder consisted of large quantities of charcoal and would have burned fiercely, rather than exploding. The Chinese possibly used these first gunpowders either as a terror weapon or to start fires.

•983 CANAL LOCK *China*
Unless a canal follows a level route, it must have locks (small compartments with double gates) at intervals. Shipping going downhill enters the full lock; closing the upper gates and emptying the lock allows the ship to sail out at the lower level. The 965-km (600-mile) long Grand Canal in China was the first to have real locks.

WORLD EVENTS

800–924

- **800** Aboriginal cultures are well established in Australia.
- **850** In Kaldi, East Africa, a goatherd notices that his flock becomes more lively after eating berries from a bush. He has discovered coffee.
- **860** The Cyrillic alphabet comes into use in eastern Europe. The alphabet has 43 letters.

Aboriginal storytellers

- **900** Islamic medicine flourishes: at Baghdad hospital a Persian physician distinguishes between the symptoms of smallpox and those of measles for the first time.
- **900** The Mayan civilization is at its height in what is now southern Mexico. Tikal, the largest city, has a population of about 100,000.

925–1049

- **950** Córdova, a Moorish city in Spain, becomes the European centre of learning.
- **1000** Viking Leif Ericsson is blown off course from Greenland, and lands on what he calls "Vinland". This is probably Newfoundland or Nova Scotia, making him the first European to visit North America.

Mayan temple

- **1000** In West Africa, the Ghanaian Empire is at the peak of its power. An Arab explorer describes the King of Ghana as "the wealthiest of all kings on the face of the Earth".
- **1000** In Central America, Mayan centres are invaded by the Toltecs, who occupy their temples.

1050

Early stained glass used only small red and blue panes. Advances in glass-making technology during the 13th century increased the range of colours and size of panes available.

·1065
STAINED GLASS
Obscure
The original function of stained glass in windows was to filter out the heat of the sunlight entering a building. The precise date when stained glass was first made is uncertain, but the earliest surviving example is from 1065 in Augsburg Cathedral, Germany, where biblical characters are depicted in five stained-glass windows.

A stained-glass window pane

Chinese characters indicating points of compass

South Pole

Rotating magnetic needle had pointer at the south-seeking end

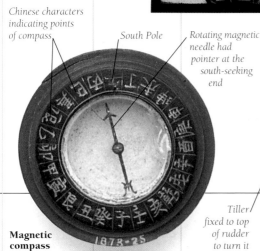

Magnetic compass

1090·
MAGNETIC COMPASS *China, Arabia*
A floating magnetized needle always points in the same direction. The magnetic compass, based on this principle, literally changed the known world: it made long-distance ocean navigation possible, and as a navigational aid it was invaluable to early explorers.

1175

Truly clear glass was difficult to make, so early magnifying glasses were slightly tinted.

Magnifying glass, 17th century

·1200
MAGNIFYING GLASS *England*
Bishop of Lincoln, Robert Grosseteste was the first to suggest using glass lenses to magnify small objects. He also anticipated the telescope, still nearly 350 years in the future, commenting that it would "…make small things placed at a distance appear as large as we want…".

Lines drawn in on roof give real impression of depth to the room

The *Apparition at the Chapter House at Arles* by Giotto, 1296

c.1290
EARLY PERSPECTIVE *Italy*
The technique of creating a realistic sense of depth and space was unknown to early artists whose scenes were largely two-dimensional. They would show table-tops, for example, at crockery-shattering angles. An early sense of perspective evolved with the work of Italian painter Giotto. He used light, shade, and colour to make his scenes more life-like.

·1286
SPECTACLES *Italy*
The first spectacles were reading glasses; the Venetian glass makers who ground the lenses called them "little discs for the eyes".

Spectacles, 17th century

A longbow is the same length from end to end as the archer's height.

c.1250
TINPLATE *Bohemia*
In the mid 13th century, Bohemia (now the Czech Republic) had one of the most advanced metal-working regions, with access to rich tin deposits. Bohemian metal workers were the first to use a coating of tin to stop iron from rusting. They used this tinplate process to protect armour.

Arabic ship with rudder

Tiller fixed to top of rudder to turn it

1180·
RUDDER *Arabia*
Since the invention of the boat, mariners had guided their vessels with the aid of an oar, or a "steer board". Steering became easier with the introduction of the rudder, which was fixed to the stern of the ship and controlled by the tiller – a horizontal bar on the top. The exact date of their invention is uncertain, but evidence of rudders in use can be seen in pictures of the Crusades, or Holy Wars, towards the end of the 12th century.

Archer using a Welsh longbow

1250–1300
LONGBOW *Wales*
Towards the end of the 13th century, Welsh archers gave the traditional bow extra power by making it longer. In battle it was much quicker to load and fire than the crossbow, and more powerful than the short bow, which it replaced.

·1280
CANNON *China*
By about 1280, Chinese engineers had learned how to use a metal barrel to aim the explosive power of gunpowder at their enemies. They had invented the first cannons.

1050–1149

·**1054** Chinese astronomers notice a new star (a supernova – exploding star) which for three weeks is bright enough to be seen in daylight, and cast a shadow at night. European astronomers do not notice it.
·**1066** William of Normandy defeats an English army at the Battle of Hastings.

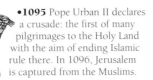

·**1095** Pope Urban II declares a crusade: the first of many pilgrimages to the Holy Land with the aim of ending Islamic rule there. In 1096, Jerusalem is captured from the Muslims.

Detail from the Bayeux tapestry depicting the Battle of Hastings

1175–1299

·**1180** In Cambodia the Angkor Empire is at its height.
·**1185–1333** Rise of the Samurai warriors in Japan during the Kamakura period.
·**1187** Islamic leader Saladin recaptures Jerusalem from Christian forces. Further European crusades fail to win back the city.

Angkor dancers

·**1266** Under the command of Kublai Khan the Mongol Empire stretches from Germany in the west to Korea in the east.
·**1271** Traveller Marco Polo leaves Venice at the start of his incredible journey to China.
·**1293** An earthquake in Japan kills 30,000 people.

1300–1779 Printing and the spread of ideas

IN THE CENTRE OF EUROPE, in the mid 15th century, a German goldsmith borrowed some money and began to print books. In his printing works, Johannes Gutenberg brought together four important inventions: moveable type, paper, ink, and the press. Individually, none of these was a new idea. Moveable type came from China, as did paper, which had only just started to replace animal-skin parchment in the West. The ink was oily paint that artists began using more than 50 years earlier, and farmers had been using presses to squeeze oil from olives for centuries. But the combination of these four technologies in printing had far-reaching effects.

Before printing, books were mostly handwritten in monasteries. They were often in Latin, so only educated people could read them, and they were so precious that some libraries kept them on chains. The printing press changed all this: a printer produced more pages in an hour than a monk could copy in a week.

The spread of ideas

The first printed books were Bibles; however, it was not long before translations of ancient Greek and Roman literature were published. Scientific books were being printed as early as 1469, such as Pliny's *Natural History*, an encyclopaedia-like collection that this Roman scholar wrote in AD 77. Medical books followed, and in the 16th century, printers set to work on new texts about modern science and technology.

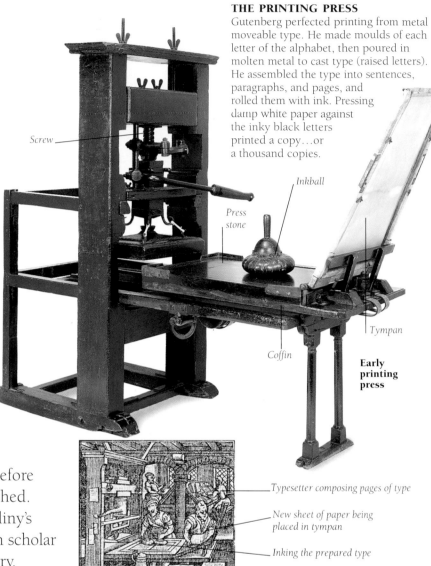

THE PRINTING PRESS
Gutenberg perfected printing from metal moveable type. He made moulds of each letter of the alphabet, then poured in molten metal to cast type (raised letters). He assembled the type into sentences, paragraphs, and pages, and rolled them with ink. Pressing damp white paper against the inky black letters printed a copy...or a thousand copies.

Screw

Inkball

Press stone

Tympan

Coffin

Early printing press

Typesetter composing pages of type

New sheet of paper being placed in tympan

Inking the prepared type

The printers' studio

THE CHANGING WORLD: 1300–1779

GUN POWER
Gunpowder was invented in China in around 950, but was not used for firing guns and cannons until around two centuries later. The deadly new firearms that appeared during the 15th and 16th centuries totally changed the nature of war, because it became easier and easier to destroy buildings and kill large numbers of people. These Swiss soldiers are heavily armed with both hand guns and cannons.

SCREW THREAD
The invention of the screw is an essential mechanical advance. First used in olive presses in ancient times, in the 15th century, the screw found new use in printing presses and in metal wood fastening.

OPTICAL DISCOVERIES
The invention of magnifying lenses and optical instruments such as the telescope and microscope gave people a new insight into nature and the heavens. The observations these tools made possible led to extraordinary advances in human knowledge.

Robert Hooke's magnification of rock crystal, 1665

Using a telescope, people could study the night sky

NAVIGATION
New developments in navigational instruments, such as the compass and later the sextant and octant, gave sailors confidence to embark on long sea voyages and explore more of the world.

Portuguese caravel, 15th century

Some of the earliest practical books were on engineering, mining, and metalworking. Books by Italian Vanocchio Biringuccio and German Georgius Agricola spread knowledge that eventually increased the production and use of metals. The replacement of wooden machines by metal ones revolutionized the technology of the time, making possible the vast range of inventions and devices that followed.

The rise of European civilization

Technology and society changed ever more rapidly in this period and a new class of people – merchants – emerged. For centuries the focus of life in Europe had been the countryside and farming. Under the feudal system, most of the land had been owned by abbeys and powerful barons, while poor people lived in conditions of near-slavery.

But as the European population rose, towns grew, and trade flourished. In the towns, merchants bought and sold goods, using their increased wealth to finance larger ventures. International trade increased via major ports, such as Venice, often with several merchants sharing the high cost of risky sea voyages. These changes laid the foundations of a banking and finance system.

As the power of the merchants grew, the influence of the old authorities, especially the Church, weakened. The new merchant class provided a ready market for books, and literacy (the ability to read) spread more widely. With literacy came free thinking: the people of Europe began to question the world around them. A most dramatic example of this spreading of knowledge came in 1543, when a Polish scholar, Nicolaus Copernicus, published *On the Revolutions of the Heavenly Spheres*. In it he suggested that the planets were in orbit around the Sun. This radical idea challenged the accepted view of the Earth as the centre of the universe. Though they lived a century apart, Copernicus and Gutenberg had turned the universe inside out. The world was never the same again.

THE PROCESS OF INVENTION

INVENTION IN EARLY TIMES

Since ancient times, craftspeople were the main inventors, gradually modifying and improving the things they made. The process – more like evolution than invention – was encouraged by craft guilds, which were organizations that trained workers and provided a framework for passing on skills from one generation to the next. Though the guilds were partly responsible for the gradual perfection of existing tools and machines, they perhaps discouraged the sudden "good ideas" and dramatic discoveries that we associate with invention today.

Metal workers from a 15th-century manuscript

EUROPE LEARNS FROM CHINA AND ISLAM

Between 1300 and 1779, Europe benefited from growing contact with the Far East and with the Islamic world, where science and technology were more advanced than in the West. European contact with Arab technology began during the Crusades (wars waged between the 11th and 14th centuries by the Christian Church against Islamic powers in the Holy Land). After the Crusades, growing international trade continued to spread knowledge to Europe. Much Chinese technology, such as the ship's rudder, reached Europe via the world of Islam. Europeans copied the rudder from Arab sailors, who had in turn seen the idea on Chinese vessels. Other Chinese ideas, such as lock gates and the wheelbarrow, may have come directly overland from China with traders transporting goods along the ancient Silk Road.

Travelling between Europe and the Far East, explorers such as Marco Polo helped spread ideas

BANK NOTES
The introduction of the first printed paper money in Europe in the 17th century meant that people no longer had to carry piles of heavy metal coins around with them. The new "promise to pay" is fundamental to a commercial system.

The clock tower in St. Mark's Square, Venice

MEASURING TIME
The first accurate mechanical clocks were introduced during the 14th century. As clocks became more common, appearing on church towers for all to see, people began to rely on them to order their day.

Samuel Crompton's mule was invented in 1779 to make spinning more efficient

MECHANIZATION OF MANUFACTURE
During the 18th century, life began to change as machines, such as Kay's flying shuttle and Hargreaves' spinning jenny, were introduced into factories to speed up production of textiles. Instead of working on looms at home, people began to move to towns to find work in industry. This was the start of industrialization.

SMELTING IRON WITH COKE
Iron production greatly increased following the invention of a way of smelting iron in a blast furnace. Iron works such as this one at Coalbrookdale, in England – the first to use a blast furnace – provided the metal needed to make the new tools and machines.

1300

1366

COUNTING & COMMUNICATION

c.1300 ESCAPEMENT CLOCK *Europe*

For regular time-keeping, a clock must include a mechanism that marks out exactly equal periods of time. The first clocks to do this began to appear around 1300. They kept time using a verge – a horizontal bar that swung back and forth. The movements of the bar trapped and released the clock's gear wheels at constant intervals. These early clocks were not fully accurate: they had to be reset each day using a sundial and they did not have a minute hand.

1350–1400 ALARM CLOCK *Germany*

Soon after mechanical escapement clocks came into use, German clock makers began to experiment with mechanical alarm clocks. It is perhaps not surprising that monks were among the first customers: they had to rise early for prayers. A monastery clock from Nuremberg, Germany dating from about 1380, has raised knobs on its dial, which enabled sleepy monks to read the time in the dark by touch. It woke them with a ringing bell, just like a modern alarm, at the pre-set time.

Mechanical clock with alarm attachment, Germany, c.1580

As the clock dial revolves, these raised bars catch the train hanging from the bell and cause it to strike.

Escapement clock, 1450

Jan van Eyck was among the first painters to really take advantage of the reflective properties of oil glazes.

Right panel of Ghent altarpiece – detail from an oil painting by Jan van Eyck, 1432

DAILY LIFE & HEALTH

c.1400 OIL PAINTING *Various*

The use of linseed oil to stick pigments to canvas was not a 15th-century invention. However, Italian Cennino Cennini's treatise of 1390 on oil paints served to popularize their use around 1400. Of the many artists to experiment with oils, Jan van Eyck of Bruges, Belgium was the first to really master oil painting, using it to create rich detail.

AGRICULTURE & INDUSTRY

1300–1350 LACE
Belgium, France

Objects resembling lace bobbins have been found in Roman remains, but there are no records of Roman lace-making. The craft of making lace may have begun in the early 14th century in Flanders (an area now on the borders of Belgium and France) and the purchase of 12,000 pins for the wedding outfit of an English princess in 1347 suggests that her dress was trimmed with lace at this time. Lace was a luxury until machines to do the work were invented in the 19th century.

Lace trimming like this was used to decorate clothes or church vestments.

Handmade lace, Italy, 16th century

•1405
SCREW *Germany*
There is some evidence of wood-screws in use in 1405, but they were not common for a further two centuries. Early screws were costly because they were made by hand. They became popular for fixing wood only when their mass-production brought prices down in the 18th century.

1421•
PATENTS *Italy*
By applying for patents, inventors disclose details of their work in exchange for protection against unauthorized copying. This system encourages the spread of knowledge, while guarding the inventor's interests.

TRAVEL & CONQUEST

c.1350
HAND CANNON *Europe*
By the mid 14th century, guns resembled miniature cannons attached to a wooden stock. They could be carried, but their size and weight made them difficult to fire from the hand. Instead, the soldier would hold the stock and prop up the muzzle of the gun, perhaps on a forked stick. (Later models had a lug, or hook, near the muzzle.) To discharge the weapon, a soldier placed a hot coal or wire through the touch hole to light the gunpowder inside. Hand cannons did not develop to handguns until the 16th century.

1411•
TRIGGER *Germany*
By the early 15th century, the crude hand cannon had developed an S-shaped trigger, called a serpentine, to hold a glowing taper. A soldier could now aim the gun by looking along the barrel: to fire, he pushed up a handle on the stock, which lowered the taper into the charge of powder.

Smooth-bore hand cannon, c.1490

Muzzle

This gun is 1.23 m (4 ft ½in) long.

Wooden stock — *Touch hole* — *Iron smooth-bore barrel*

Hook to help lodge the gun in a wall and to take the recoil, or force, of the shot.

WORLD EVENTS

1300–1365

• **1300** The population of the world is about 360 million.
• **1300** Around this time the Anasazi people who built the remarkable Cliff Palace at Mesa Verde, Colorado, abandon the settlement and go south.
• **1325** Arab traveller Ibn Battuta sets off on the first

Palace of Mesa Verde

of several trips through the Islamic world and beyond. He goes as far as India, Spain, and sub-Saharan Africa.
• **1337–1453** The Hundred Years' War is fought between France and England.
• **1347** Rats on ships arriving at European ports spread bubonic plague. The deadly disease kills almost half the population of Europe.

1366–1430

• **1386** In England, Geoffrey Chaucer starts to write *The Canterbury Tales*.
• **1400** In Siberia, northeast Asia, the body of a woolly mammoth is found preserved in ice. It is at least 30,000 years old.
• **1415** The Chinese send fleets to visit Indian Ocean ports. In return, the bustling African city-state of

Woolly mammoth

Malindi sends a giraffe to the emperor of China.
• **1418** Portuguese Prince Henry the Navigator sponsors sailors on expeditions around the African coast, starting a process of discovery that will lead eventually to the colonization of America.

1431　　1495

1450•
PRINTING PRESS *Germany*
Johannes Gutenberg and his partner played a large part in perfecting the technology of moveable type. By rolling the letters with an oil-based ink, they were able to print the first European books. The biggest contribution they made to history was perhaps the press. They adapted a linen press to make it faster to operate and more suitable for printing books. *See* **MOVEABLE TYPE 1040**.

Gutenberg Bible, printed in 1455

c.1450
CONCAVE LENSES
Germany
A concave lens is thinner at the middle than at the edges. German scientist and philosopher Nicholas of Cusa was the first to realize that such a lens could be used in spectacles to correct short-sightedness.

1450•
CLOSED-EYE NEEDLE
Netherlands
China was the only source of simple metal needles for many years. Needle makers of the Netherlands invented the modern steel needle with a fully formed eye in the 15th century.

1470–1480
MARINER'S ASTROLABE *Europe*
Since the 3rd century BC, astronomers have been using astrolabes – circular maps of the heavens. Between 1470 and 1480, European navigators adapted the astrolabe for mariners' use. They discarded the star map and turned it into a simple navigational instrument for measuring the latitude of lands and locations at sea.

Circular scale

Rotating arm with eyeholes and pointer

c.1500
SHIRT *Europe*
The hip-length shirt as a visible garment appeared only at the end of the 15th century, when the men's fashion for open-necked doublets (sleeveless jackets) with slashed sleeves revealed it. Formerly, men wore undershirts, but the tunic, or gypon, concealed them.

Slashes in the doublet reveal the shirt beneath.

•1504 ETCHING *Germany*
The well-dressed knight in the early 16th century wore decoratively engraved armour. To cut down the amount of work involved in doing this, armourers began to use an acid etching process. They waxed the armour, scratched tiny lines in it and allowed the acid to do the work of engraving. Later they realized that they could make printing plates for etched pictures.

Decorative etching

Italian armoured breastplate, 1570

•1509
WALLPAPER *England*
The oldest surviving fragment of wallpaper, dating from 1509, was produced by printer Hugo Goes of England. The paper decorated the ceiling of the Master's Lodge at Christ's College, Cambridge.

Hand-painted wallpaper, France, 1780

•1530 BOTTLE CORK *France*
The individual bottle of wine was unknown before the 16th century. Instead, wine was stored in barrels or vats. The introduction of bottle corks meant that wine could be stored in bottles without air getting in and souring it. The first reference to a bottle cork occurs in *Leclaircissement de la Langue Francoyse* by John Palsgrave, 1530. They were widespread by the 17th century. Without corks, the invention of champagne would not have been possible. *See* **CHAMPAGNE 1670**.

One of the first pieces of diving equipment was this strange bell-shaped arrangement of leather and metal.

Leather straps

•1538
DIVING BELL *Spain*
The first diving bells were simple cylinders that were open at one end. Lowering them into water with the open end down retained the air, so that anyone inside could work under water until the oxygen ran out. The first detailed accounts of experiments with diving bells date from 1538, when a bell was in use in Spain.

Cock
Pyrites
Wheel
Trigger

This pistol has three of these wheel-lock mechanisms so it can fire three successive shots without reloading.

Barrel

1520•
WHEEL-LOCK TRIGGER MECHANISM *Europe*
The wheel-lock trigger mechanism for firing a gun was invented around 1520. On pulling the trigger, a serrated wheel rotates against a chunk of iron pyrites causing a shower of sparks that discharge the gun. Wheel-lock guns were expensive and intricate weapons.

Triple wheel-lock pistol, Germany, 1550

1528•
GRENADE *France*
An explosive earthenware "bomb" caused injuries in a battle between French and Spanish armies in 1528. This is the first recorded evidence of grenades.

Soldier carrying a grenade

1431–1494

•**1431** English forces occupying parts of France execute the French leader, Joan of Arc, by burning her at the stake.
•**1438** The Inca Empire begins to expand in the Andes Mountains, in the region that is now Peru in South America. Powerful Inca armies conquer their weaker neighbours.

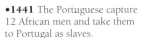

Inca knife

•**1441** The Portuguese capture 12 African men and take them to Portugal as slaves.
•**1456** Vlad the Impaler comes to power in what is now southern Romania. His cruelty is the origin of the blood-drinking Dracula legend.
•**1492** Christopher Columbus sails from Spain, heading for India.

1495–1559

•**1503** Italian artist Leonardo da Vinci starts to paint the Mona Lisa.
•**1518** A Spanish slave ship sails from Africa to America. Over three centuries, European slave traders ship more than 11 million people across the Atlantic.
•**1519** Explorer Hernan Cortés takes Mexican chocolate back to Spain. It enters the Spanish diet as a drink.

•**1540** Under Suleiman the Magnificent, the Turkish Ottoman Empire reaches the height of its power. The Ottomans control a large area – Egypt, Syria, the Arabian Peninsula, and parts of southern Europe.

Suleiman the Magnificent

1560

1585

1560	1565	1570	1575	1580	1585	1590	1595	1600

COUNTING & COMMUNICATION

c.1565
PENCIL *Various*
Swiss physician and naturalist Konrad von Gesner described the use of a writing instrument resembling a pencil in 1565. In 1795, pencils became more common when French mechanical genius and painter Nicholas Conté discovered a practical method of making pencil lead: grinding graphite with clay, forming it into sticks, and baking them.

1594•
LOGARITHMS *Scotland*
Logarithm tables are a practical way of multiplying and dividing large numbers. To multiply, the mathematician looked up the logarithm of each number in the table, then added the "logs" to get the logarithm of the answer. John Napier, a Scottish mathematician, had the idea of logarithms in 1594, but it took him many years to perform the calculations needed to compile his tables. They were finally printed in 1614.

Napier's logarithm tables, 1614

As temperature rises, alcohol expands and is pushed up into the coiled glass tube. The level it reaches indicates the temperature.

DAILY LIFE & HEALTH

•1560
CONDOM *Italy*
The linen condom was first used as a way of avoiding disease but its value in preventing pregnancy was recognized within a century. By 1800, condoms made of sheep gut were in common use. These were dried, and had to be soaked in water before use. The famous Italian lover Casanova called condoms "English overcoats" and recommended tying them in place with pink ribbon.

Oil reservoir for flame

Eyepiece

Water in sphere focuses light of flame on specimen

Hooke's compound microscope, 1660

Plant specimen

c.1590
COMPOUND MICROSCOPE *Netherlands*
In 1590, Dutch spectacle maker Hans Janssen and his son put two lenses at opposite ends of a tube, and used them to examine tiny objects. They had created the first compound microscope. However, few people used a microscope until English scientist Robert Hooke improved the instrument 75 years after its invention.

•1592 THERMOMETER *Italy*
Italian Galileo Galilei used a tube of air dipped in a container of coloured liquid to make the first crude thermometer. As the trapped air warmed and expanded, it pushed the liquid level down. More precise sealed alcohol thermometers relied on the expansion of the fluid itself. They came into use around 1660.

c.1590 TELESCOPE *Obscure*
The origins of the refracting telescope – a telescope containing lenses rather than mirrors – are obscure. In 1608, Hans Lippershey, a Dutch spectacle maker, is said to have put two lenses together and looking through them noticed that a distant rooftop appeared enlarged. In 1634, Hans Janssen described how he had copied an Italian telescope dating from 1590. Whoever invented the instrument, Galileo was the first to apply it for serious astronomical observation in 1609.

This would be filled with alcohol.

Replica of an Italian alcohol thermometer of 1660

AGRICULTURE & INDUSTRY

Object lens magnifies subject, but inverts it (turns it upside down)

•1568 SCREW-CUTTING LATHE *France*
French court inventor Jacques Besson was probably the first to build a practical screw-cutting lathe, for making screws around 1568.

1589•
KNITTING MACHINE *England*
William Lee, an English clergyman, built the first knitting machine around 1589, using sets of hooked needles like those on modern knitting machines. He made little progress promoting his machine, because hand-knitters opposed its introduction fearing that it would spoil their chances of getting work.

Knitting machine in use

Replica of Galileo's telescope

Eyepiece lens turns image the right way up

Cock

Steel plate

Flint

TRAVEL & CONQUEST

Mercator projection map of the world, 1569

Tortoiseshell veneer

Butt

•1569
MERCATOR PROJECTION MAP *Germany*
When geographers first tried to map large areas, they found that copying the Earth's curved surface on to flat paper always distorted direction or distance. To make their maps as accurate as possible, they used a technique called projection. In 1569, mathematician and engineer Gerhardus Kremer, known as Mercator, devised a greatly improved projection which is still named after him. It allowed navigators to plot an accurate course anywhere on the globe.

•1589 DREDGER *Netherlands*
Dredgers – vessels that remove mud and weeds from waterways – were invented in 1589. By the 19th century, steam power had improved their efficiency.

Pulling the trigger releases the cock causing flint to strike steel and create sparks, which ignite the gunpowder.

WORLD EVENTS

1560–1584

•**1565** Muslims destroy the Indian city of Vijayanagar, capital of the Hindu empire in southern India.
•**1568** With the aid of guns provided by European missionaries, warlord Oda Nobunaga takes control of Kyoto, and starts a series of victories over his opponents that will eventually unite Japan.

Potato plant

•**1573** Spanish explorers returning from Peru introduce a native South American vegetable, the potato, to Europeans.
•**1580** Fear and persecution of witches reaches a height in Europe, resulting in the torture and killing of thousands of innocent women.

•**1588** English battleships led by Francis Drake defeat the Spanish Armada – a fleet sent by King Philip II to invade England.
•**1590** English playwright William Shakespeare begins to write his first works for the stage.
•**1598** Missionaries continue their destruction of the African

Kabuki theatre

peoples' culture and religion: in the Congo, West Africa, they convert King Affonso to Christianity, and he orders his people to burn their idols.
•**1600** The population of the world is about 545 million people.
•**1603** Kabuki theatre begins in Japan.

1610

1635

| 1610 | 1615 | 1620 | 1625 | 1630 | 1635 | 1640 | 1645 | 1650 | 1655 |

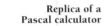

Slide rule, 1654

1622•
SLIDE RULE *England*
By tracing logarithms on to a pair of rulers, mathematician William Oughtred invented a rapid way of multiplying and dividing. His calculating device was called a slide rule.

•1623 CALCULATOR *Germany*
Wilhelm Schickard of Tübingen was perhaps bored with taking his socks off to count to numbers above ten when he invented an adding machine, or simple calculator, in 1623. The machine has not survived, but its mechanism was probably similar to the gear-driven calculator built by Frenchman Blaise Pascal some 20 years later.

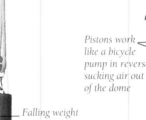

1656•
PENDULUM CLOCK *Netherlands*
Dutch mathematician and astronomer Christiaan Huygens revolutionized time-keeping with his first practical pendulum clock. The pendulum, which regulated the hands, swung so regularly that the clock was accurate to five minutes a day. Earlier instruments gained or lost up to an hour a day.

Model of a pendulum clock made by Huygens in 1673

Replica of a Pascal calculator

Answers appear here

Numbers to be added or subtracted are dialled here.

Pump creates a vacuum in this glass dome

Pistons work like a bicycle pump in reverse, sucking air out of the dome

c.1610 BAGELS *Poland*
The bagel – a firm, ring-shaped bread roll – may be a Polish invention: Jewish community regulations of Cracow in 1610 refer to pregnant women receiving an extra ration of bagels.

1637•
UMBRELLA *France*
"Three umbrellas of oiled cloth… trimmed with gold and silver…" appear in a 1637 list of the possessions of King Louis XIII of France. This is the first reference to a waterproof umbrella: earlier versions were sunshades. (The name umbrella comes from the Italian word *ombrello* meaning "little shade".) Waterproof umbrellas were not widely used until the late 19th century.

Falling weight drives hands round

c.1620
MERRY-GO-ROUND *Obscure*
The origins of this old fairground amusement are hard to trace. It may have been a Turkish invention. An early reference to it comes from records of a Turkish fair held in 1620. Within a century, merry-go-rounds were popular throughout Europe.

French merry-go-round, 1680

This weight acts as a counter balance.

Francis Hauksbee's improved vacuum pump, 1709

1650–1654
VACUUM PUMP *Germany*
Physicist Otto von Guericke built the first pump to suck air, rather than water. With it he created a vacuum in the space between two half spheres. The pressure of the air outside pressed the hemispheres tightly together. His pioneering work made the invention of the atmospheric steam engine possible (*see* **1712**).

Regular swing of pendulum ensures clock keeps correct time

German flintlock pistol, c.1660

Leather washers sealed the oar holes, yet allowed for rowing.

Wooden submarine, 1683

•1610 FLINTLOCK FIRING MECHANISM *France*
Around 1610, a new firing mechanism began to appear on hand guns – the flintlock. On pulling the trigger, a shaped flint flew forward, striking a steel plate and showering the powder-filled pan with sparks to fire the gun. Flintlock guns were more convenient to use than matchlocks and more reliable and cheaper than wheel-locks. However, they did not become popular until some 30 years after their invention.

•1624 SUBMARINE *England*
Dutchman Cornelius Drebbel was working for English King James I when he built the first submarine. It had a greased leather skin stretched over a wooden frame. Although the submarine leaked badly, the 12 oarsmen inside succeeded in rowing it along London's River Thames at a depth of about 4 m (13 ft).

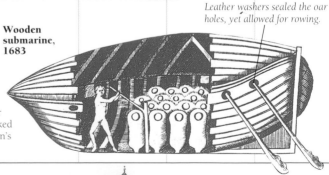

1610–1634		1635–1659	

•**1615** English people begin to drink tea, a novelty introduced from British colonies in eastern Asia.
•**1616** Many native Americans die in New England in an epidemic of smallpox, introduced by European settlers.
•**1616** The Roman Catholic Church bans a book by Nicolaus

The Mayflower

Copernicus for suggesting that the Earth moves round the Sun.
•**1620** The *Mayflower* arrives at Cape Cod, America with pilgrim settlers from Europe.
•**1628** English physician William Harvey proves that the heart pumps blood endlessly round the body.

•**1639** The Tokugawa rulers of Japan isolate their nation from the rest of the world: foreigners are restricted to trading posts at Nagasaki.
•**1648** The Mogul emperor of India, Shah Jahan, completes the Taj Mahal at Agra. He builds it as a temple and a memorial to his empress, Arjumand Banu Begu.

Taj Mahal

•**1649** Oliver Cromwell rules the Commonwealth (republic) of England, Scotland, and Ireland after the execution of the English King Charles I.
•**1650** Settlers in New England, America begin to hunt whales in the coastal waters near their colonies.

1660   # 1680

1660	1664	1668	1672	1676	1680	1684	1696

COUNTING & COMMUNICATION

The value of this bank note is marked here – 100 dalers.

Swedish bank note from 1666

•1670 MEGAPHONE *England*
The voice-amplifying potential of a cone-shaped tube seems to have first occurred to Englishman Sir Samuel Morland, the master mechanic to English King Charles II. He is said to have invented the megaphone in 1670.

•1675 POCKET WATCH *Netherlands*
Christiaan Huygens not only invented the pendulum clock, he also devised a way of putting accurate time in our pockets. He improved existing portable clocks (invented by German Peter Henlein around 1500) by being one of the first to add a spring to the balance wheel, which made more reliable watches possible. The first of his clocks to include a balance wheel was made in Paris in 1675: it was accurate to within two minutes a day.

As it turns, the balance wheel tightens the coil spring attached to it, which repeatedly reverses the direction of rotation.

Pocket watch with spring balance

DAILY LIFE & HEALTH

•1661 BANK NOTE *Sweden*
Paper money was a Chinese invention. The government printed the notes. It wasn't until the 17th century that banks started to do this: the first was the bank of Stockholm, Sweden.

•1670 CHAMPAGNE *France*
A French monk is generally credited with the invention of champagne wine in 1670. Dom Pérignon discovered that by bottling and tightly corking wine while it was still fermenting, he could make it fizzy. The wine "tasted like stars" according to the tippling monk, and to this day the traditional champagne cork has a star on it.

•1683 PRECISION MICROSCOPE *Netherlands*
A Dutch instrument maker, Anton van Leeuwenhoek, was the first to make high-powered precision microscopes. Though they only had one tiny lens, they were capable of far greater magnification and produced much clearer and more precise images than earlier models. His instruments could magnify a specimen by 200 times, enabling him to sketch bacteria. *See* COMPOUND MICROSCOPE 1590.

Screw to adjust position of specimen

Leeuwenhoek's precision microscope

Pin for holding specimen

A single, powerful lens is held between two plates. Compound microscopes have several lenses.

1690–1700 CLARINET *Germany*
Nuremberg instrument maker Johann Christoph Denner is said to have invented the clarinet during the last decade of the 17th century, though similar instruments had been in use for many years, in the form of the chalumeau. The clarinet was the first instrument in which the reed was completely covered by the player's lips.

Early 18th-century clarinet, Germany

AGRICULTURE & INDUSTRY

•1660 UNIVERSAL JOINT *England*
The universal joint holds two parts securely together yet permits movement in all directions. Englishman Robert Hooke made the first universal joint for a telescope. With it he could support the instrument rigidly, yet point it anywhere in the sky. Since then, universal joints have been widely used in a number of machines, including the motor car transmission.

Rotating upper component also turns lower one

Cross piece hinges in two directions

One of Hooke's drawings of a universal joint

Lower and upper portions are linked, yet can turn to any angle.

Water is sucked up from flooded floor of mine and is forced out at the surface.

Savery's steam pump, 1698

1698• STEAM PUMP *England*
Engineer Thomas Savery used a simple steam machine to drain flooded mines. It sucked up floodwater as steam condensed in its cylinder, forming a vacuum. Closing valves and letting more steam in then forced the water out of the cylinder and up the mine shaft.

A worker below ground kept the boiler fire alight and operated the valves of the "water-raising machine".

TRAVEL & CONQUEST

•1662 OMNIBUS *France*
The omnibus (the forerunner of today's bus) became popular only in the 19th century. Long before that, in the 1660s, French mathematician Blaise Pascal and his partners are said to have launched a horse-drawn bus service around Paris. Unlike the rural stagecoach, the omnibus was designed specifically for city use. Pascal's service used seven vehicles, each seating eight, and the buses eventually ran on five routes.

Horse-drawn omnibus

WORLD EVENTS

1660–1679

- **•1666** The Great Fire destroys most of London. Many buildings are rebuilt using stone, rather than wood.
- **•1667** First recorded successful blood transfusion is carried out in France, using the blood of a lamb.
- **•1675** A slave costing 30 florins in Africa fetched 10 to 15 times as much in North America.

Chrysanthemum

- **•1676** Danish astronomer Ole Christensen Römer measures the speed of light for the first time.
- **•1678** French missionary and explorer Louis Hennepin is the first European to see North America's Niagara Falls.
- **•1678** The Japanese chrysanthemum flower is introduced to Europe.

1680–1699

- **•1680** Pueblo tribes in the Rio Grande river area of North America drive out Spanish missionaries who are trying to convert them to Catholicism. They also destroy most of the Spanish churches there.

- **•1682** English astronomer Edmond Halley watches a bright comet, and predicts (correctly) that it will return 76 years later.

Edmond Halley

1700

1700 | 1704 | 1708 | | | 1724 | 1728 | 1732

1704–1709
ORRERY *England*
English instrument builder George Graham made the first orrery between 1704 and 1709. The machines got their name from the Earl of Orrery, who had one built around 1712. An orrery was a clockwork model of the universe showing the Earth's changing position throughout the year. It was not the first machine to simulate the heavens: the Ankythera machine, found near Crete, suggests that people used mechanics to predict the movements of heavenly bodies as long ago as 80 BC.

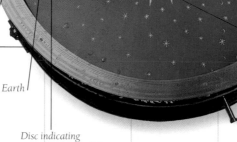

Sun

Moon

Earth

Disc indicating time around the globe

Winding handle to turn orrery

•1731
OCTANT *England*
In 1731, Englishman John Hadley and American Thomas Godfrey of Philadelphia independently invented a new navigational instrument – the octant. It used twin mirrors to align an image of the Sun or a star with the horizon and determine latitude (distance north or south); its great advantage was that the ship's motion did not affect observations.

Mirror reflects Sun

Sight hole

Scale

Octant, c.1750

c.1700 PIANO *Italy*
Italian harpsichord maker Bartolomeo Cristofori built the first piano around the start of the 18th century. Felt-covered hammers struck its strings to play notes. The player could vary the loudness of the notes, from *piano* – soft – to *forte* – loud. Its predecessor, the harpsichord, lacked such expressive possibilities.

Piano, England, 1773

Pushchair-style prams like this were popular from around 1840.

•1733
PERAMBULATOR *England*
In 1733, English architect William Kent designed a perambulator, or pram, for the 3rd Duke of Devonshire's children. Shaped like a shell, it was made to be drawn by a dog or a Shetland pony.

Perambulator, c.1840

Counter weights drive caisson down

Winch for raising buckets of rubble

Airlock

Air pump

Model of a caisson, 1851

1709•
IRON SMELTING – COKE *England*
By the 18th century, much of Europe's woodland had been felled to fuel furnaces that made iron. At his iron works in Coalbrookdale, Abraham Darby found a way of making iron using coal instead of wood. He roasted the coal to drive off impurities and make coke, which he then used as a fuel for his blast furnaces.

•1712
ATMOSPHERIC STEAM ENGINE *England*
The first steam-powered piston engine, built by Thomas Newcomen, should correctly be called an atmospheric engine. Steam filled the cylinder of the pumping engine, but it was atmospheric pressure which pushed in the piston as a spray of cold water condensed the steam, creating a vacuum.

Newcomen's steam engine, 1712

1738•
PNEUMATIC CAISSON *England*
Swiss engineer Charles de Labelye's caisson solved the problems that builders faced when digging bridge foundations. The caisson used pressurized air to force water away from an area of river bed so that work could proceed on "dry" underwater land.

•1733
FLYING SHUTTLE *England*
John Kay's flying shuttle device halved the labour needed to weave cloth, so textile manufacturers were quick to adopt it. This made Kay so unpopular with weavers that he fled to France, where he died a poor man.

Beam pulls mine pump rod up as piston in engine goes down

Water supply for spray

Rod leads down mine shaft to operate a water pump below ground draining flood water

Cylinder with piston inside

Boiler

Puckle's machine gun

•1718 MACHINE GUN *England*
Ever since the invention of the gun, engineers had tried to find ways of firing many shots in rapid succession. The first to do so was James Puckle, who patented a machine gun in 1718. His unique machine was a financial failure. Later machine guns were more successful, especially the Gatling and Maxim guns. American Hiram S. Maxim made a fortune from a water-cooled machine gun used to devastating effect in World War 1.

1700–1719

•**1700** The population of the world is about 610 million.
•**1707** The Act of Union brings together England and Scotland as the United Kingdom.
•**1707** With the death of Aurangzeb the Mogul dynasty (India's ruling group), weakens after nearly two centuries of power. Over the next 150 years, the Moguls gradually lose authority to the English colonists.
•**1710** Meissen porcelain factory opens in Dresden, Germany.
•**1717** German composer George Frederick Handel writes his Water Music to entertain the English king's river party.

Meissen factory workers

1720–1739

•**1720** In France the "Mississippi bubble" bursts. Shares in Louisiana settlements plummet and speculators who have invested in them lose everything.
•**1721** The population of the Japanese city of Edo (now Tokyo) rises to more than 1 million.

Diamonds found in Brazil

•**1727** House rats from Siberia appear in Europe for the first time.
•**1729** Gems found in Brazil, South America, are identified as diamonds, starting a rush to the Minas Gerais region.
•**1737** The world's second-largest recorded earthquake kills 300,000 people in India.

1740 1750

| 1740 | 1742 | 1744 | 1746 | 1752 | 1754 | 1756 | 1758 |

COUNTING & COMMUNICATION

•1742 CENTIGRADE TEMPERATURE *Sweden*
Swedish astronomer Anders Celsius devised the temperature scale that bears his name. The scale is also, and more commonly, known as centigrade. He set the boiling and freezing points of water as 0 and 100 respectively. This temperature scale was later adopted in many countries as part of the metric system *See* METRIC SYSTEM 1791–1795.

18th-century French thermometer

Copy of Harrison's fourth chronometer, 1795

Sextant

1759•
MARINE CHRONOMETER *England*
To judge how far they travelled west or east and calculate longitude, mariners noted when the Sun was overhead compared to the time of noon at their home port. Accurate clocks were thus essential for navigation, and in 1714 the English Board of Longitude offered a cash prize to anyone who could make one. In 1759, Englishman John Harrison succeeded in making an accurate marine clock, or chronometer. It was tested over a period of years on several voyages and was found to be accurate to 30 seconds a year, even on a storm-tossed ship.

Mirror

•1757 SEXTANT *England*
In 1757, John Campbell adapted the octant to create the sextant, which was more accurate. When used with a chronometer, the sextant enabled sailors to measure their exact position at sea. *See* OCTANT 1731.

Telescopic lens

DAILY LIFE & HEALTH

This thermometer has details of record temperatures marked on it: it says here that in 1742, the French city of Lyons reached 15 degrees below zero centigrade (-15°C).

Mass of water would create slight head of pressure.

Ivory scale

Using a sextant, a navigator could determine longitude at sea by looking at the position of the Moon in relation to the stars. An octant was useless when the Moon was in certain parts of the sky.

This lightning conductor's tip has been bent by intense heat.

AGRICULTURE & INDUSTRY

•1741 CARBONATED WATER *England*
Physician William Brownrigg is believed to have been the first to prepare carbonated, or soda, water in 1741. He did this by forcing carbon dioxide gas through still water, and bottling it. English experimenter Joseph Priestley made carbonated water some 30 years later by dissolving gas from a brewing vat in water.

•1743 SHEFFIELD SILVER *England*
Cutlery maker Thomas Boulsover was repairing a knife when he noticed that heat and pressure made a piece of silver stick to copper firmly. He then began to make silver-plated copper buttons which looked as if they were solid silver. His workshop was in Sheffield so the process became known as Sheffield silver.

Carbonated water apparatus, 1767

Carbonated water is drawn off here

•1752 LIGHTNING CONDUCTOR *North America*
In 1752, American statesman and scientist Benjamin Franklin demonstrated that lightning was a form of electricity by flying a kite in a storm. The kite line conducted electricity to a metal key tied on it near the ground. Sparks flying from the key showed the electric charge. This led him to invent the lightning conductor to protect buildings in storms.

TRAVEL & CONQUEST

Set of Sheffield silver-plated spoons

Carbon dioxide gas is passed through here and bubbles up through water.

A thick wire connects this spike on top of the building to the ground. When lightning strikes the spike, the wire conducts the electricity harmlessly to the ground.

Lightning conductor

WORLD EVENTS

1740–1749
•**1740** Laws discriminating against black American slaves make racial prejudice official. A typical law from Virginia made black slaves the... "chattel (property) personal in the hands of their owners and possessors ... for all intents, construction, and purpose whatsoever".

Bering enters strait

•**1741** Danish navigator Vitus Bering discovers the strait between Russia and Alaska, which is now named after him.
•**1747** English naval surgeon James Lind shows that fresh citrus fruit can prevent scurvy – the disease that killed sailors on long ocean voyages.

1750–1759
•**1750** The population of the world is about 720 million people.
•**1752** A change to the calendar in Britain and America shifts the date forward. This causes riots because people believe they are being robbed of 11 days' life.

Covered wagon

•**1753** Pennsylvania Dutch settlers in Conestoga introduce a covered wagon that would be widely used for transport across the prairies.
•**1759** French writer Voltaire publishes his novel *Candide*, in which he pokes fun at the fashionable idea that "everything is for the best".

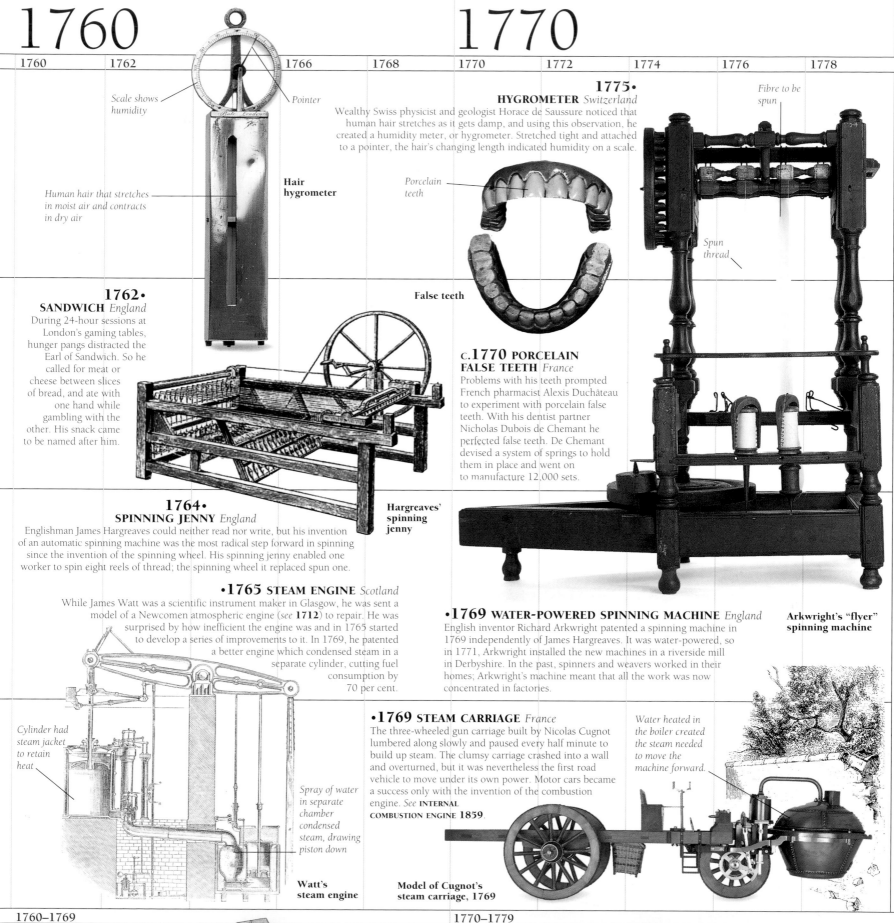

1760

1770

Scale shows humidity

Pointer

Human hair that stretches in moist air and contracts in dry air

Hair hygrometer

1775•
HYGROMETER *Switzerland*
Wealthy Swiss physicist and geologist Horace de Saussure noticed that human hair stretches as it gets damp, and using this observation, he created a humidity meter, or hygrometer. Stretched tight and attached to a pointer, the hair's changing length indicated humidity on a scale.

Fibre to be spun

Porcelain teeth

Spun thread

False teeth

1762•
SANDWICH *England*
During 24-hour sessions at London's gaming tables, hunger pangs distracted the Earl of Sandwich. So he called for meat or cheese between slices of bread, and ate with one hand while gambling with the other. His snack came to be named after him.

c.1770 PORCELAIN FALSE TEETH *France*
Problems with his teeth prompted French pharmacist Alexis Duchâteau to experiment with porcelain false teeth. With his dentist partner Nicholas Dubois de Chemant he perfected false teeth. De Chemant devised a system of springs to hold them in place and went on to manufacture 12,000 sets.

Hargreaves' spinning jenny

1764•
SPINNING JENNY *England*
Englishman James Hargreaves could neither read nor write, but his invention of an automatic spinning machine was the most radical step forward in spinning since the invention of the spinning wheel. His spinning jenny enabled one worker to spin eight reels of thread; the spinning wheel it replaced spun one.

Arkwright's "flyer" spinning machine

•1765 STEAM ENGINE *Scotland*
While James Watt was a scientific instrument maker in Glasgow, he was sent a model of a Newcomen atmospheric engine (*see* **1712**) to repair. He was surprised by how inefficient the engine was and in 1765 started to develop a series of improvements to it. In 1769, he patented a better engine which condensed steam in a separate cylinder, cutting fuel consumption by 70 per cent.

•1769 WATER-POWERED SPINNING MACHINE *England*
English inventor Richard Arkwright patented a spinning machine in 1769 independently of James Hargreaves. It was water-powered, so in 1771, Arkwright installed the new machines in a riverside mill in Derbyshire. In the past, spinners and weavers worked in their homes; Arkwright's machine meant that all the work was now concentrated in factories.

Cylinder had steam jacket to retain heat

•1769 STEAM CARRIAGE *France*
The three-wheeled gun carriage built by Nicolas Cugnot lumbered along slowly and paused every half minute to build up steam. The clumsy carriage crashed into a wall and overturned, but it was nevertheless the first road vehicle to move under its own power. Motor cars became a success only with the invention of the combustion engine. *See* **INTERNAL COMBUSTION ENGINE 1859.**

Water heated in the boiler created the steam needed to move the machine forward.

Spray of water in separate chamber condensed steam, drawing piston down

Watt's steam engine

Model of Cugnot's steam carriage, 1769

1760–1769

•**1762** Native American religious leader The Delaware Prophet starts to urge his followers in the Ohio Valley to return to traditional ways and abandon European things. Many take his advice.
•**1764** Austrian composer Wolfgang Amadeus Mozart composes his first symphony, aged eight.

Mozart

•**1769** Englishman James Cook sails around New Zealand, and up the east coast of Australia in his ship the *Endeavour*. He finds the "southern continent" he is seeking.
•**1769** The world's worst famine kills about 10 million Indians in Bengal (now Bangladesh).

1770–1779

•**1773** In a tax protest, American colonists board British ships in Boston Harbour and tip cargoes of tea overboard. This becomes known as the Boston Tea Party.
•**1776** Thomas Jefferson drafts the Declaration of Independence to formally cut links with Britain, and create the United States of America.

Declaration of Independence

•**1777** French chemist Antoine Lavoisier shows that oxygen and nitrogen are the main components of air.
•**1779** In southern Africa, Boers (Dutch colonists) clash with native Africans of the Xhosa tribe. This fighting continues for years as white settlers keep taking the best farmland.

1780–1869 Steam power and the industrial revolution

WATER, WIND, AND MUSCLE powered almost all machines until the mid 18th century. But suddenly a new power source emerged that was to change the face of industry for ever: steam. Able to work tirelessly at jobs that quickly exhausted humans or animals, steam did not depend on the weather or the flow of a stream. As people took advantage of steam to power new, larger, more mechanized factories, green fields were filled with mill chimneys, and sleepy hamlets turned into smoky cities.

How steam developed

The earliest steam engines were pumps used to suck water from mines. The first was built in 1712 by English blacksmith Thomas Newcomen to drain water from mines in Cornwall, southwest England. Half a century passed before manufacturers found other uses for the steam engine. But in 1762, steam engines began to fan the furnaces of iron foundries and to work hammers. Production of iron soared, and the cost fell by half. This in turn affected almost all aspects of industry. With plenty of metal, engineers could replace wooden components with stronger, more efficient iron parts.

However, the real stimulus to industry came in 1784 with the development by Scottish inventor James Watt of steam engines that could turn wheels. Watt was famous for his improvements to the steam pump, and he perfected his rotary engines just as change was sweeping through other industries. Textile mills in particular were changing fast. Samuel Crompton's "mule" had made

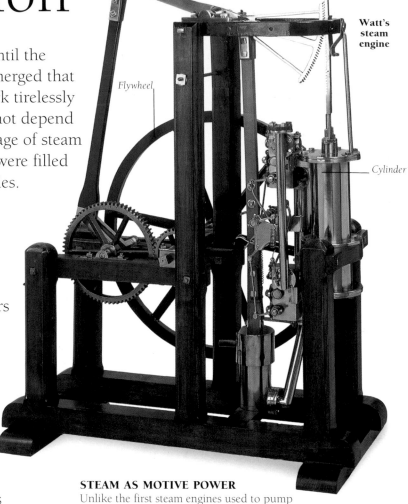

Beam

Watt's steam engine

Flywheel

Cylinder

STEAM AS MOTIVE POWER
Unlike the first steam engines used to pump water from mines, Watt's engine produced circular motion, which could be used instead of water power to drive the new factory machines. As a result, factories and the machines in them grew in size, and productivity increased. The new engines were soon put to use to power railway locomotives, heralding the steam era.

THE CHANGING WORLD: 1780–1869

A reproduction of Robert Stephenson's "Rocket" locomotive, 1829

STEAM TRAINS
The first passenger steam trains went into service in the 1830s, making cheap, rapid travel available to all but the poorest people. In Europe, the new railways were made to serve existing cities, but in the USA the railways themselves created many towns, opening up the relatively empty interior. By 1869, people could cross the vast continent from east to west by rail.

COMMUNICATION
Investors using the earliest electric telegraphs took advantage of their advance knowledge of business markets to buy and sell shares at the best prices. But communication by telegraph did not become international until inventors found a way of linking continents by undersea cables.

London stock market scene, 1852

PHOTOGRAPHY
With the invention of photography in 1827, people could, for the first time ever, see real-life images of far-off places, people, and events – without travelling there. This early photograph, taken around 1855, shows the cook house of the 8th Hussars during the Crimean War. The photographer was Roger Fenton, who is recognized as one of the first photo-journalists.

spinning more efficient in 1779, and later inventions speeded weaving. These machines, at first powered by muscle or water, transformed fabric-making from a cottage craft to a factory job. With one of Watt's rotary engines, mill owners could build factories far from water, and use steam power in place of a water wheel. Steam power also made bigger factories possible. Transport networks developed to bring in raw materials and take away finished goods. Roads improved, and new canals halved the cost of transporting heavy goods like coal. The invention of the steam train in the early 19th century led to the construction of a web of railway lines. The big factories attracted workers from the countryside, and cities grew quickly. In 1801, only 14 European cities had populations of 100,000; 70 years later, more than 100 cities were this big. City life was grim for the new class of industrial workers: housing and sanitation were bad, and factory wages low.

The spread of industrialization

Industrialization began in Britain but soon spread to Europe and the USA. American industrialization, however, followed a rather different course. European machines relied on a large supply of cheap, skilled operators, while US machines sought to make more expensive workers more productive. One US machine could often do the jobs of several European workers. American engineers also aimed to mass-produce goods by manufacturing them with parts that were interchangeable. The parts of two rifles made by traditional craft methods may look alike, but if different parts broke on each gun, the remaining good parts would not fit together. If the guns had interchangeable parts, though, you could make a working gun from the two broken ones.

Making interchangeable parts was at first difficult and costly, but it was much more efficient. Together with automation, it became known as the "American System" of manufacturing and gave the USA a lead in industry – just as the industrial revolution in Europe was slowing down.

THE PROCESS OF INVENTION

THE PATENT SYSTEM

By the 18th century, the patent system, which had begun in Italy in 1421, was widespread and its increasing use encouraged invention. Inventors disclosed full details of their work in a patent application. On approval of the idea by the government patent office, an account of the invention was published, so protecting it from being copied for a fixed number of years – typically 16. Patents stimulated invention in three ways: they informed people of the latest technology; inventors had time to profit from their ideas before they were copied; and, by limiting the period of protection, the patent system ensured that good ideas would eventually benefit everybody, not just the inventor.

Patent model of Whitney's cotton gin

WARFARE FUELS INVENTION

Warfare has always stimulated invention. The first war of the industrial age, the Crimean War (1853–56), provoked a surge of weapons patents – and it is not hard to see why. Weapons inventors needed to sell their idea to just one wealthy customer – the government. If successful, they could also be sure of enormous orders. One inventor who grasped the advantages of military technology was American-born engineer Hiram S. Maxim, whose water-cooled machine gun is remembered long after his other inventions – including a better mousetrap – were forgotten. Skills learnt making weapons may also affect nonmilitary technologies. Metal-working techniques improved as foundries struggled to make stronger gun barrels. And it is no coincidence that the costly technology of interchangeable parts first appeared in the manufacture of rifles.

Hiram S. Maxim's water-cooled machine gun

MEDICAL ADVANCES

During the 19th century, new methods of preventing and curing disease were discovered, which gave people a better chance of survival than in previous centuries. New equipment, such as the stethoscope, enabled doctors to know what was happening inside the body, while antiseptics and anaesthetics made surgery safer. This picture shows the first surgical use of Morton's ether inhaler – a kind of anaesthetic – in Boston, USA, in 1846.

FARMING

As more and more people gave up their land to work in towns, the demand for mass-produced food increased. More efficient farming methods were sought and agriculture gradually became more mechanized. Artificial fertilizers made it possible to grow large expanses of crops. Farmers cut their fields with new, labour-saving reaping machines, such as the one above, which was invented in the USA by Cyrus McCormick in 1831.

ROAD TRANSPORT

The invention of the bicycle brought with it better roads and new technologies, many of which, such as pneumatic tyres, were later used in the manufacture of motor cars. Bicycles provided people with a cheap and independent form of transport – and a brand new leisure activity!

A demonstration of early bicycles

MASS-PRODUCTION

Though costly, the factory system and interchangeable parts made it possible to manufacture large numbers of goods. In the mass-production of muskets, inspectors carried gauges like these from armoury to armoury to check that each dimension of each piece of a gun was correct – and interchangeable with all the other similar pieces.

1780

1780	1783	1786	1789	1792

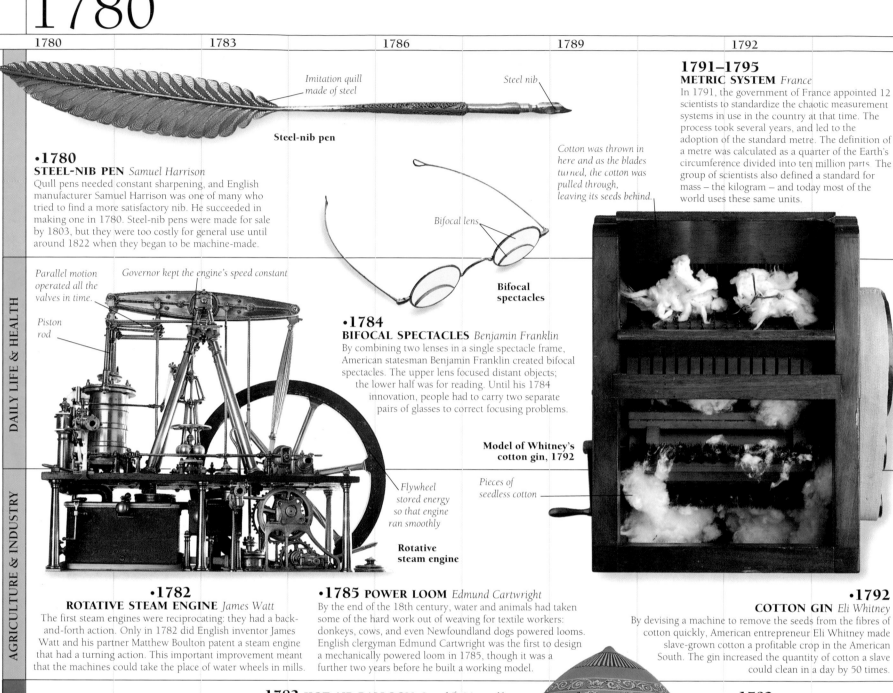

Imitation quill made of steel

Steel nib

Steel-nib pen

•1780
STEEL-NIB PEN *Samuel Harrison*
Quill pens needed constant sharpening, and English manufacturer Samuel Harrison was one of many who tried to find a more satisfactory nib. He succeeded in making one in 1780. Steel-nib pens were made for sale by 1803, but they were too costly for general use until around 1822 when they began to be machine-made.

Cotton was thrown in here and as the blades turned, the cotton was pulled through, leaving its seeds behind.

Bifocal lens

Bifocal spectacles

•1784
BIFOCAL SPECTACLES *Benjamin Franklin*
By combining two lenses in a single spectacle frame, American statesman Benjamin Franklin created bifocal spectacles. The upper lens focused distant objects; the lower half was for reading. Until his 1784 innovation, people had to carry two separate pairs of glasses to correct focusing problems.

1791–1795
METRIC SYSTEM *France*
In 1791, the government of France appointed 12 scientists to standardize the chaotic measurement systems in use in the country at that time. The process took several years, and led to the adoption of the standard metre. The definition of a metre was calculated as a quarter of the Earth's circumference divided into ten million parts. The group of scientists also defined a standard for mass – the kilogram – and today most of the world uses these same units.

Parallel motion operated all the valves in time.

Governor kept the engine's speed constant

Piston rod

Model of Whitney's cotton gin, 1792

Flywheel stored energy so that engine ran smoothly

Pieces of seedless cotton

Rotative steam engine

•1782
ROTATIVE STEAM ENGINE *James Watt*
The first steam engines were reciprocating: they had a back-and-forth action. Only in 1782 did English inventor James Watt and his partner Matthew Boulton patent a steam engine that had a turning action. This important improvement meant that the machines could take the place of water wheels in mills.

•1785 POWER LOOM *Edmund Cartwright*
By the end of the 18th century, water and animals had taken some of the hard work out of weaving for textile workers: donkeys, cows, and even Newfoundland dogs powered looms. English clergyman Edmund Cartwright was the first to design a mechanically powered loom in 1785, though it was a further two years before he built a working model.

•1792
COTTON GIN *Eli Whitney*
By devising a machine to remove the seeds from the fibres of cotton quickly, American entrepreneur Eli Whitney made slave-grown cotton a profitable crop in the American South. The gin increased the quantity of cotton a slave could clean in a day by 50 times.

Parachute descent

•1783 HOT-AIR BALLOON *J. and É. Montgolfier*
In 1782, two French paper makers, Joseph and Étienne Montgolfier, noticed that they could make a silk bag float in the air by filling it with smoke. In 1783, they publicly demonstrated a hot-air balloon made of silk and lined with paper, which rose to 1,830 m (6,000 ft). Later that year they launched the first hot-air balloon with two passengers. The balloon flew 9 km (5½ miles) across Paris.

•1783
PARACHUTE DESCENT *Louis Lenormand*
The ancient Chinese may have known the principle of the parachute. Italian Renaissance artist Leonardo da Vinci certainly suggested its use, in his book *Codex Atlanticus*, but Frenchman Louis Lenormand made the first descent in a parachute. He jumped from a tree, and then from a tower in the French town of Montpellier in 1783.

Model of the Montgolfiers' hot-air balloon

•1792 AMBULANCE
Dominique-Jean Larrey
In the late 18th century, Baron Dominique-Jean Larrey was famed for his speed as an army surgeon (he amputated 200 limbs in a single battle). Today he is better remembered as the inventor of the ambulance. He introduced a light, well-sprung vehicle that could be harnessed to a pair of horses to replace the hand-drawn carts that had previously bumped wounded soldiers painfully to field hospitals.

DAILY LIFE & HEALTH

AGRICULTURE & INDUSTRY

TRAVEL & CONQUEST

WORLD EVENTS

•**1782** In Peru, native peoples led by Tupac Amaru revolt against Spanish rule. A war is waged, ending in victory for the Spaniards.
•**1783** By signing the Treaty of Paris, Britain recognizes the independence of the United States of America, and the Revolutionary War ends.

•**1788** Britain begins to punish criminals by transporting them to Australia, where they live in harsh conditions with little food.
•**1789** Social revolution begins in France. Joseph Guillotin suggests using a humane machine to behead condemned aristocrats. This machine – the guillotine – is named after him.

The French guillotine

•**1791** In China, *Dream of the Red Chamber* by Ts'ao Chan is published. Its vivid descriptions of Chinese society make it a popular novel.
•**1792** English writer and feminist Mary Wollstonecraft writes *A Vindication of the Rights of Women*, demanding that women be educated as well as men, and have the same rights.

1795

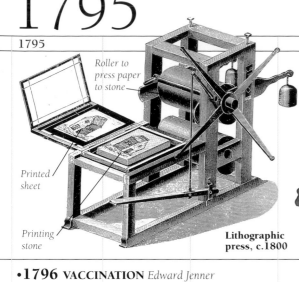

Roller to press paper to stone

Printed sheet

Printing stone

Lithographic press, c.1800

•1798 LITHOGRAPHY *Alois Senefelder*
When German Alois Senefelder was writing out a laundry list in 1796, he discovered a method of printing – lithography – that is now universal. He found that the words, which were scribbled on a polished limestone slab in a waxy ink, repelled water but attracted oily printing ink. By wetting, then inking the stone, Senefelder could print copies of the list. He developed the process for printing music, and later it was used for illustrations.

Lamp glasses needed frequent cleaning to remove soot.

Lighting a 19th-century gas street lamp

Piling up many pairs of plates increased the voltage of the battery

Copper and zinc plates

Rods powered by the pistons drove all four wheels

•1796 VACCINATION *Edward Jenner*
In 1796, English doctor Edward Jenner deliberately infected a boy with cowpox, then, when he was well again, exposed him to smallpox. The boy did not catch smallpox, because the milder illness had made him immune. Similar methods of vaccination are used today to protect people from killer diseases.

This model was used to demonstrate how the hydraulic press worked and how it could be used to break wooden boards and iron bars.

•1802 GAS COOKER
Zachaus Andreas Winzler
Early gas enthusiast Zachaus Winzler manufactured the new fuel at his home in Austria, and piped it to the kitchen, where he was probably the first to use it for cooking. By giving a series of dinner parties in 1802, he tried to popularize gas cookers. However, these did not become common until the end of the century

•1807 STREET GAS LIGHTING *England*
Experimenters first lit buildings with gas in 1785, but few followed their lead because the gas smelt revolting. In the open air, though, the smell was not a problem, and in 1807, Britain's National Light and Heat Company demonstrated the first street lights in London, close to where Buckingham Palace now stands.

The locomotive's heavy boiler broke the track when it first ran.

Pump action of handle moved piston up slowly, but with great force

Model of a hydraulic press, c.1866

•1796 HYDRAULIC PRESS *Joseph Bramah*
English cabinet maker Joseph Bramah was the first to make practical use of hydraulic (fluid-pressure powered) machinery. In his hydraulic press, gentle pressure on a small piston forced water into a much larger cylinder. The increased pressure moved a piston in the large cylinder a tiny distance, but with greater force.

Volta's pile – the first battery

•1800 BATTERY *Alessandro Volta*
While skinning dead frogs in an anatomy lesson, a pupil saw one of them twitch. Alessandro Volta demonstrated that the steel scalpel and the zinc work bench had formed a simple electric cell, and the cell's current had made the frog's muscles contract. Following these principles, Volta made the first battery. It was a pile of zinc and copper plates interleaved with brine-soaked cloth.

**1803 •
RAILWAY LOCOMOTIVE** *Richard Trevithick*
English engineer Richard Trevithick invented a railway locomotive in 1803, but this first engine was virtually ignored. His second attempt incorporated two revolutionary advances. Firstly, it had smooth steel wheels, which gripped the flat metal rails tightly (everyone thought they would slip); secondly, by directing exhaust steam up the chimney, Trevithick fanned the locomotive's fires. In 1808, he was commissioned to build a railway locomotive to demonstrate the power of steam. It was called "Catch-me-who-can" and the inventor exhibited it on a circular London track in an effort to raise funds.

Model of Trevithick's "Catch-me-who-can" locomotive

•**1795** Scottish explorer Mungo Park sets out to search for the source of Africa's River Niger.
•**1799** The Rosetta Stone is found in Egypt. The various languages carved on it enable historians to translate two forgotten ancient Egyptian scripts.

Mungo Park starts his expedition

•**1800** With a population of 1.5 million, Canton in China is the world's largest city. It is nearly twice the size of London, Europe's largest population centre at this time.
•**1803** The US government buys the Louisiana Territory from the French.
•**1804** Slave rebellion in Haiti leads to overthrow of French rule. Haiti becomes the second independent American nation after the USA.

Napoleon Bonaparte

•**1804** In France, Napoleon Bonaparte, commander of the French Revolutionary armies, crowns himself emperor.
•**1807** The British government makes trading in slaves illegal. The USA bans their import from Africa the following year.

1810

1815

1810	1811	1812	1813	1814	1815	1816	1817	1818

Magnifier to read scale

Prism separates light into spectrum

Beam of light passes through here

Today spectroscopes are often used for chemical analysis. Every element burns with a flame of a different colour, so heating a substance and examining the flame with a spectroscope reveals its composition.

This end is narrow so sounds are funnelled to the ear.

Light from source enters here

Eyepiece

Divided circle allows wavelength to be measured

Telescope to view spectrum

Hollow wooden tube

19th-century spectroscope

Stethoscope, c.1830

DAILY LIFE & HEALTH

•1811
CANNED FOOD *Nicolas Appert*
Complaining about army food has been a military tradition ever since there have been armies. The French government recognized the problem by offering a cash prize for a means of supplying high-quality food to the troops. In 1811, Nicolas Appert won it by heating food in glass jars and sealing the tops with cork. Later, he replaced the jars with tin cans, somewhat similar to those used today.

Food being sealed in tin cans

•1814 SPECTROSCOPE
Joseph von Frauenhofer
In 1802, scientist William Wollaston used a slit and prism to spread out and study the spectrum (rainbow colours) of sunlight. He noticed black lines crossing his rainbow. Some 12 years later Joseph von Frauenhofer added a telescope to the prism and slit and made what is now called a spectroscope. Through the work of scientists using this instrument we now know that the black lines in the spectra of the sun and stars indicate their chemical contents.

•1816 STETHOSCOPE *René Laënnec*
French physician René Laënnec thought of the idea for a stethoscope while watching children playing. If one child scratched a wooden plank, another could hear the scratches far away by pressing an ear against the wood. Laënnec then used a hollow wooden tube to listen to the chests of his patients and learned to recognize the sounds of healthy and sick bodies. American physician George P. Cammann designed the modern two-ear model in the early 20th century.

AGRICULTURE & INDUSTRY

•1812
HYDRAULIC JACK
Joseph Bramah
By patenting the hydraulic jack in 1812, Joseph Bramah was the first to use pressure power for lifting, rather than pressing (*see* **HYDRAULIC PRESS 1796**). Hydraulic jacks similar to Bramah's are still used today in garages to lift cars.

The first tin cans were so securely sealed that they had to be opened with a hammer and chisel.

•1815
MINER'S SAFETY LAMP
Humphry Davy
Investigations of explosions in coal mines revealed that the cause was "firedamp" (an explosive gas) ignited by the flame in miners' lamps or candles. English chemist Sir Humphry Davy experimented with the gas, and in 1815 he produced a safety lamp in which gauze enclosed the oil flame. The flame could not ignite the firedamp, and burned brighter when the dangerous gas was present. Davy's lamp allowed mine owners to open deeper pits, but tragically, this eventually led to even more deaths because the mines were not adequately ventilated.

•1818
TUNNELLING MACHINE
Marc Brunel
To tunnel under London's River Thames, French-born engineer Brunel created a cast iron shell as big as the tunnel, made in segments. A labourer stood in each segment and dug forwards with a spade, while those behind him removed the soil, and lined the tunnel with bricks. As the tunnel grew, the shield was inched forward.

Davy lamp

TRAVEL & CONQUEST

Hammer strikes percussion cap of cartridge to fire gun

•1818
REVOLVER
Elisha Collier, Artemis Wheeler
Numerous inventors tried to speed up the rate of fire of a hand gun by pre-loading several shots in a rotating cylinder. All "revolvers" are based on this idea, the most popular containing six shots. Two Americans, Elisha Collier and Artemis Wheeler, both patented revolvers in 1818, and Collier's guns sold well. Yet another American, Samuel Colt, simplified the cocking mechanism and mass-produced the weapons from 1836. Colt's name has been linked to the "six-shooter" revolver ever since.

This end is round to collect sounds from the patient's chest.

Revolving cylinder containing six chambers to hold six cartridges, hence the name six-shooter

Colt revolver, 1851

1816–1820 MACADAMIZED ROADS *John McAdam*
Scottish inventor John McAdam devised a method of improving road surfaces. "Macadamized" roads were raised and well-drained, built from crushed stone and gravel. The addition of tar, a waste product of the growing gas industry, from the 1830s onwards improved the process still further.

WORLD EVENTS

1815–1819

A Luddite

•**1810** The ruler of Hawaii, Kamehameha, conquers the last large islands in the group. White traders provide the firearms that make this possible.
•**1811** In England, gangs of textile workers, nicknamed Luddites, smash the weaving and spinning machines that are taking their jobs.

•**1812** The USA declares war on Britain because of a dispute over borders and trade. The war lasts nearly three years and achieves very little.
•**1812** The German Grimm brothers, Jacob and Wilhelm, write a collection of fairy tales, including Hansel and Gretel.

•**1815** The British East India Company, which already rules the Indian mainland, takes control of Sri Lanka from the Dutch.
•**1816** In Africa, Shaka becomes king of the Zulus. By conquering neighbouring tribes, he creates a great Zulu nation that fights European colonists in southern Africa.

Zulu King Shaka

•**1817** Work begins on the Erie Canal, linking New York City to the American Great Lakes. Better transport increases settlement there.
•**1819** The *Savannah* becomes the first steamship to cross the Atlantic, though it uses steam only for 90 hours of the month-long crossing, relying on sail power for the rest.

1820 1825

Set of imperial measures

1824•
IMPERIAL MEASURES *British government*
As in France, traders in 19th-century Britain had to cope with a bewildering range of measurement units. For length, they could choose from: palms, Gunter's links, spans, feet, cubits, paces, poles, perches, chains, and more. To simplify the system, British Parliament passed a weights and measures act in 1824, which defined all measurement in "Imperial Units" based on the yard and pound. *See* **METRIC SYSTEM 1791**.

1827•
PHOTOGRAPHY *Joseph-Nicéphore Niépce, Louis Daguerre*
The invention of photography required a lens, a camera obscura, and a light-sensitive material. Niépce, a Frenchman, was the first to bring these components together. He formed his image on a bitumen-covered pewter plate; washing the plate in lavender oil removed the tar where it had not been hardened by the action of light. His partner, Daguerre, perfected the daguerreotype photographic process 12 years later.

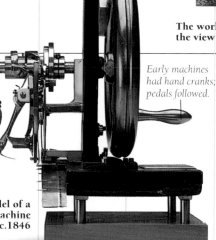

The world's earliest existing photograph – the view from Niépce's window, c.1827

Machine-made pins, c.1870

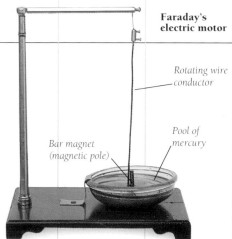

This rotates to move pins from grinder to polisher and then head maker

Patent model of John Howe's pin-making machine, 1832

Patent model of a pioneer sewing machine by Elias Howe, c.1846

Early machines had hand cranks; pedals followed.

1829•
SEWING MACHINE *Various*
A French tailor, Barthélemy Thimonnier, patented a sewing machine in 1829, but other tailors, who saw it as a threat, destroyed his workshop. Walter Hunt independently invented the sewing machine in the USA, closely followed by Elias Howe, but neither marketed their invention well. Sewing machines were not a success until Isaac Singer devised a scheme for marketing them. He hired female salespeople to offer the machines on credit or instalment plans.

•1824
PIN-MAKING MACHINE *Lemuel Wright*
In England, as early as the 1770s, pins were made by many workers, each specializing in one minute process. American labour was more expensive, and so the pin industry in the USA was mechanized first. Lemuel Wright patented a pin-making machine in 1824, but it was not until the 1840s that John Howe's machine was able to compete with hand manufacture.

•1827 WATER TURBINE *Benoît Fourneyron*
A French engineer invented the water turbine to improve the efficiency of water mills. His idea turned the mill wheel on its side, and directed the water's flow from the centre outwards through the blades. Fourneyron's turbine drove mill machinery directly, but as electric power grew in importance, water turbines were often coupled to generators.

•1821
ELECTRIC MOTOR *Michael Faraday*
In 1821, English scientist Michael Faraday demonstrated a simple device, in which a current-carrying wire rotated around a magnet; though crude, it was the first device to turn electricity into movement. Among others, American Joseph Henry produced a practical electric motor in 1831, which used direct current from a battery.

Model of McCormick's reaper, 1850s

•1826 REAPING MACHINE *Patrick Bell*
Many inventors tried to produce mechanical reapers to take the hard work out of hand reaping, but Scotsman Patrick Bell was the first to succeed, in 1826. Many miles away, American farmer's son Cyrus Hall McCormick was developing a quite different design. The McCormick reaper, which was patented five years after Bell's machine, eventually made a greater impact on farming methods.

Faraday's electric motor

Rotating wire conductor

These reels push cut grain on to the platform.

•1827
DIFFERENTIAL GEAR *Onésiphore Pecqueur*
If an axle rigidly links a vehicle's two driving wheels, cornering causes problems: the wheel on the inside must turn more slowly than that on the outside, or one of them will skid. To prevent this, all cars use a small gearbox called a differential. The ancient Chinese had a similar device, but the kind used in modern cars was invented by a Frenchman in 1827.

Platform

Bar magnet (magnetic pole)

Pool of mercury

Cut grain is taken from platform and tied in shocks

Reaper is horse-drawn from here

Cutter bar is behind here

•**1821** Napoleon Bonaparte dies in exile on the island of St. Helena.
•**1821** After three years of fighting, South Americans under Simon Bolivar win independence from Spanish rule for the state of Gran Colombia (now Colombia, Ecuador, Panama, and Venezuela).
•**1822** The discovery of a tea bush growing wild in north India ends China's control of the tea industry.
•**1822** The first of five potato crop failures in Ireland causes disastrous famines.
•**1822** The African state of Liberia is established as an attempt to send American slaves back to Africa.

South American struggles

•**1825** The success of smallpox vaccination in Japan encourages the acceptance of Western medicine, leading to a decline in traditional healing.
•**1825** Russian Czar (king) Alexander I dies after eating poisonous mushrooms.
•**1827** The people of Tennessee, USA, elect frontiersman and popular hero Davy Crockett to represent them in Congress.

Davy Crockett

•**1828** Dutch manufacturer Conrad J. van Houten prepares a new confectionery using cacao beans – the chocolate bar.
•**1829** In India, British rulers declare the custom of Suttee illegal. The ruling ends the tradition that a dead man's widow must kill herself by jumping on to his funeral pyre.

1830

1835

| 1830 | 1831 | 1832 | | 1835 | 1836 | 1837 | 1838 | 1839 |

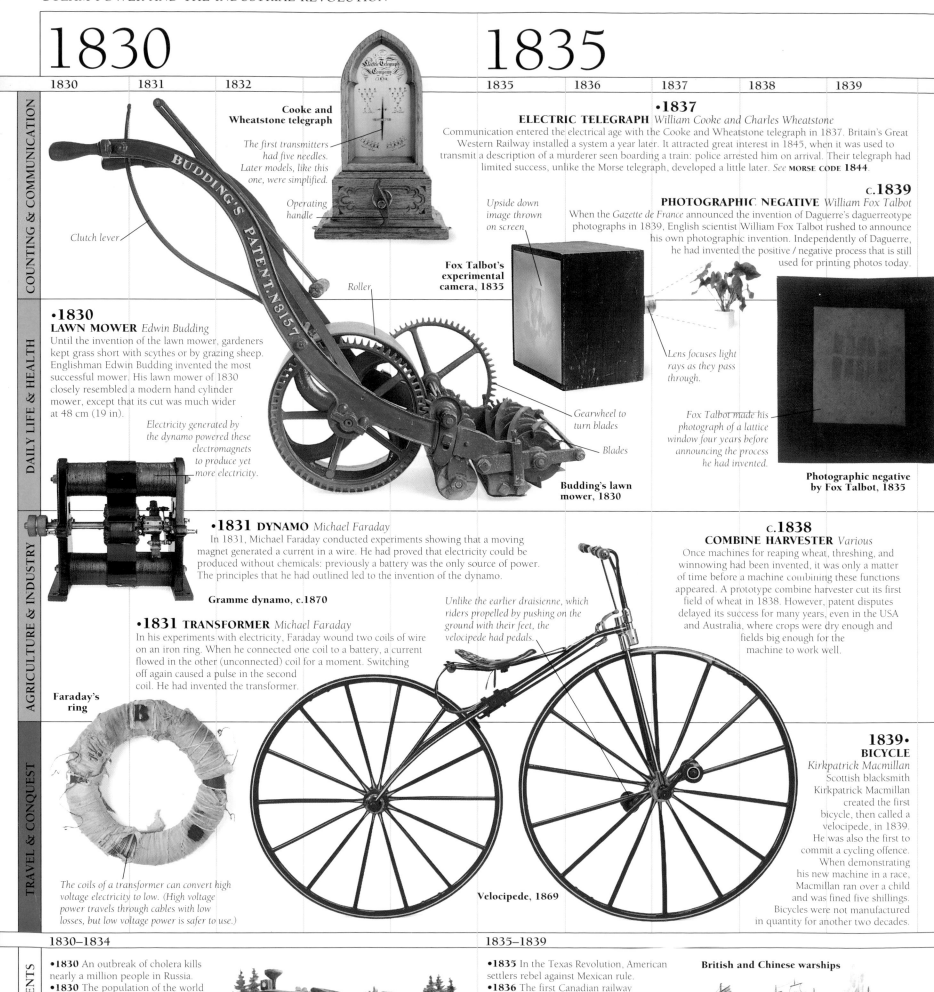

COUNTING & COMMUNICATION

Cooke and Wheatstone telegraph

The first transmitters had five needles. Later models, like this one, were simplified.

Operating handle

•1837
ELECTRIC TELEGRAPH *William Cooke and Charles Wheatstone*
Communication entered the electrical age with the Cooke and Wheatstone telegraph in 1837. Britain's Great Western Railway installed a system a year later. It attracted great interest in 1845, when it was used to transmit a description of a murderer seen boarding a train: police arrested him on arrival. Their telegraph had limited success, unlike the Morse telegraph, developed a little later. *See* MORSE CODE **1844**.

Clutch lever

Roller

DAILY LIFE & HEALTH

•1830
LAWN MOWER *Edwin Budding*
Until the invention of the lawn mower, gardeners kept grass short with scythes or by grazing sheep. Englishman Edwin Budding invented the most successful mower. His lawn mower of 1830 closely resembled a modern hand cylinder mower, except that its cut was much wider at 48 cm (19 in).

Electricity generated by the dynamo powered these electromagnets to produce yet more electricity.

Upside down image thrown on screen

Fox Talbot's experimental camera, 1835

Lens focuses light rays as they pass through.

Gearwheel to turn blades

Blades

Budding's lawn mower, 1830

c.1839
PHOTOGRAPHIC NEGATIVE *William Fox Talbot*
When the *Gazette de France* announced the invention of Daguerre's daguerreotype photographs in 1839, English scientist William Fox Talbot rushed to announce his own photographic invention. Independently of Daguerre, he had invented the positive / negative process that is still used for printing photos today.

Fox Talbot made his photograph of a lattice window four years before announcing the process he had invented.

Photographic negative by Fox Talbot, 1835

AGRICULTURE & INDUSTRY

•1831 DYNAMO *Michael Faraday*
In 1831, Michael Faraday conducted experiments showing that a moving magnet generated a current in a wire. He had proved that electricity could be produced without chemicals: previously a battery was the only source of power. The principles that he had outlined led to the invention of the dynamo.

Gramme dynamo, c.1870

•1831 TRANSFORMER *Michael Faraday*
In his experiments with electricity, Faraday wound two coils of wire on an iron ring. When he connected one coil to a battery, a current flowed in the other (unconnected) coil for a moment. Switching off again caused a pulse in the second coil. He had invented the transformer.

Faraday's ring

Unlike the earlier draisienne, which riders propelled by pushing on the ground with their feet, the velocipede had pedals.

c.1838
COMBINE HARVESTER *Various*
Once machines for reaping wheat, threshing, and winnowing had been invented, it was only a matter of time before a machine combining these functions appeared. A prototype combine harvester cut its first field of wheat in 1838. However, patent disputes delayed its success for many years, even in the USA and Australia, where crops were dry enough and fields big enough for the machine to work well.

TRAVEL & CONQUEST

The coils of a transformer can convert high voltage electricity to low. (High voltage power travels through cables with low losses, but low voltage power is safer to use.)

Velocipede, 1869

1839•
BICYCLE
Kirkpatrick Macmillan
Scottish blacksmith Kirkpatrick Macmillan created the first bicycle, then called a velocipede, in 1839. He was also the first to commit a cycling offence. When demonstrating his new machine in a race, Macmillan ran over a child and was fined five shillings. Bicycles were not manufactured in quantity for another two decades.

WORLD EVENTS

1830–1834
•**1830** An outbreak of cholera kills nearly a million people in Russia.
•**1830** The population of the world reaches about 1,000 million.
•**1832** In Britain the Reform Bill allows middle-class men to vote in parliamentary elections. The number of voters doubles, but women and working-class men are still excluded.

The first Canadian railway ran for 23 km (14 miles) and linked two towns in Quebec.

1835–1839
•**1835** In the Texas Revolution, American settlers rebel against Mexican rule.
•**1836** The first Canadian railway is completed and starts operating.
•**1839** China's attempt to prevent British merchants from trading in opium (an addictive drug) starts the first Opium War. The Chinese quickly lose and are forced to trade freely with European nations.

British and Chinese warships

1840

1845

•1840 POSTAGE STAMP
James Chalmers, Rowland Hill

In 1840, the British Post Office introduced a gummed sticker for letters which paid for delivery anywhere in Britain, regardless of distance. Scottish publisher James Chalmers suggested the use of gummed stamps, but it was Rowland Hill who started the low-cost, uniformly priced service.

1843• CHRISTMAS CARD
Henry Cole

Printed Christmas cards are quite a recent invention. The first was commissioned by English designer and writer Henry Cole. Artist John Calcott Horsley drew a family raising their glasses in a Christmas toast: a subject that caused a storm of protest from temperance (anti-alcohol) campaigners.

•1844 MORSE CODE
Samuel Morse

To transmit all the letters of the alphabet, Cooke and Wheatstone's transmitter needed five wires. American Samuel Morse reduced this to just one wire, sending letters in a code of dots and dashes. At least 62 people claimed credit for the telegraph, but it is named after Morse, who sent the first "Morse code" message from Washington to Baltimore in 1844. Joseph Henry and Alfred Vail helped him develop the system.

Stylus

Electromagnets move stylus to mark paper.

Experimental Morse code receiver, 1849

This clockwork mechanism moves paper tape.

W.T.G. Morton's ether inhaler, 1846

Glass dome is filled with sponges soaked in the anaesthetic liquid ether.

Patient inhales anaesthetic vapour through mouthpiece

Morton's inhaler was first used in surgery in 1846.

•1844 ANAESTHETICS *Horace Wells*

Without anaesthetics to make the patient unconscious, surgery was an ordeal for everyone involved. The first use of anaesthesia was in dentistry: American dentist Horace Wells persuaded another dentist to pull one of his teeth out using nitrous oxide (laughing gas) as an anaesthetic. Ether, which was more effective, came into use in about 1850.

•1846 SAXOPHONE *Antoine Sax*
Belgian Antoine (alias Adolphe) Sax patented the instrument named after him in 1846. Though made of brass, the saxophone is actually a woodwind instrument, because a vibrating reed creates the notes.

Electromagnetic mechanism

Portable micrometer

1848• MICROMETER *Jean Palmier*
A screw advances a tiny amount, known as its pitch, with each full turn; so measuring the rotation of the screw indicates its advance with a finer precision than the pitch. Frenchman Jean Palmier was the first to use this principle for accurate measurement of small objects when he introduced his screw gauge, or micrometer, in 1848.

c.1840 INTERCHANGEABLE PART MANUFACTURE *Various*
The concept of making parts interchangeable originated in France in the 1780s, but more than 20 years passed before it became practical at the factory level. Engineer Marc Brunel pioneered the process in 1808 at a British ships' block-, or pulley-making factory. In the 1830s, Simeon North of Connecticut, USA, made rifles with fully interchangeable parts, and by the 1840s the practice was commonplace.

1846–1847 ARC LAMP *W.E. Staite*
Early in the history of electricity it was clear that sparks from electric wires would produce light. In practice, creating a continuous spark, or arc, wasn't easy. Early arc lamps used carbon rods; touching the ends together started the spark, but the spark's heat then burned down the rods. W.E. Staite demonstrated the first practical arc lamps using a clockwork device to keep the rods a constant distance apart.

Arc lamp

Dismantled rifle with parts, 1855

•1846 NITROGLYCERINE *A. Sobrero*
Italian chemist Ascanio Sobrero first produced nitroglycerine in 1846. Though 13 times more powerful than gunpowder, this oily liquid at first seemed useless, because it was so unstable. Even rubbing the liquid was enough to detonate it. Alfred Nobel later tamed the explosive.
See DYNAMITE 1865.

Assembled rifle

Gap where light is produced

Carbon rods

•1845 PNEUMATIC TYRE *R.W. Thomson*
R.W. Thomson introduced the pneumatic (inflated) tyre in his patent of 1845, but the world wasn't ready for it. In 1888, Irish veterinary surgeon John Boyd Dunlop "reinvented" the tyre to make a more comfortable cycle for his son. As cycling increased in popularity, so did the pneumatic tyre.

1840–1844

•1840 In New Zealand, native Maori people surrender their power to British settlers in return for citizenship under the terms of the Treaty of Waitangi. War over land ownership follows.
•1840 In the USA, the Underground Railroad, a network of people opposed to slavery, helps escaped slaves from the southern states flee to the northern states, where slavery is illegal.
•1844 After the banning of his newspaper in Germany, socialist Karl Marx moves to Paris. His writings in the years that follow lay the foundations for Communism.

Treaty of Waitangi

1845–1849

•1846 German astronomer Johann Gottfried Galle discovers Neptune. Astronomers had already predicted the planet's existence and position, after observing how its gravity affected the orbits of other planets.
•1847 British novelist Charlotte Brontë publishes *Jane Eyre*.

California gold rush

•1847 The discovery of gold in California leads to a rush of fortune-seekers to the area, increasing the state's population tenfold in five years.
•1849 In France, physicist Armand Fizeau is the first to measure the speed of light with accuracy.

1850

1850	1851	1852	1853

COUNTING & COMMUNICATION

•1850 INTERNATIONAL SUBMARINE TELEGRAPH CABLE *Jacob and John Brett*

Once the principle of the telegraph was established, the advantages of international links became obvious. British engineers Jacob and John Brett linked Britain and France with a successful submarine (underwater) telegraph cable in 1851. A cable linking Europe and the USA followed in 1866, making communication between the two continents instantaneous at a time when the fastest ships took 11 days for the transatlantic crossing.

Rubber-like substance prevents electricity from leaking

A length of submarine cable

Copper strands

Twisted steel cables

Cross-section of submarine cable

Grippers clamp lift cabin to shaft if the cable breaks.

DAILY LIFE & HEALTH

c.1850 SAFETY MATCH
Johan Edvard Lunström

Early matches were highly inflammable, and house fires sometimes started through mice or rats chewing the match heads. Safety matches, which catch fire only when rubbed on a specially formulated striking surface, were invented in Sweden.

Strip of phosphorus reacts with match head when match is struck against it

Matches tipped with an oxidizing agent

Safety matches

•1851 OPHTHALMOSCOPE *Hermann von Helmholtz*

Anyone who has visited an optician (eye-doctor) has seen the piercing beam of the ophthalmoscope. Invented in Germany in 1851, this instrument shines a narrow beam into the patient's eye, allowing the optician to examine its inside, and to judge the degree of short- or long-sight.

1853•
HYPODERMIC SYRINGE *Charles Pravaz*

A French surgeon devised the hypodermic syringe to inject drugs directly into the body, rather than having to swallow them. His silver syringe had a screw action; piston-operated glass syringes with interchangeable needles were not produced until 1895.

Glass cylinder to hold liquid to be injected

Syringe, c.1865

•1854
ELEVATOR *Eli Otis*

Safety fears stopped elevators, or lifts, from being used for passengers until 1854. American Eli Otis changed this. He devised a gripper mechanism attached to the lift cage. Tension in the lift rope held in the grippers, so the cage travelled freely. If the rope broke, the grippers engaged with a rack in the shaft, and the lift stopped. Otis dramatically demonstrated this by standing in a lift while an axe-man cut the cable. As the audience gasped the inventor called out: "All safe…".

Paraffin burns without smoke

c.1854
PARAFFIN *Abraham Gesner, James Young*

In the 1850s most oil lamps ran on vegetable or whale oil and whales were slaughtered in large numbers to supply light. American Abraham Gesner perfected a lamp oil from asphalt rock, which he called kerosene. Around the same time in Britain, James Young developed a similar lighting fuel from heated coal, which he called paraffin.

AGRICULTURE & INDUSTRY

1851•
MODULAR BUILDING SYSTEM *England*

English gardener Joseph Paxton suggested a vast hothouse of glass and iron for London's Great Exhibition. To build it quickly, engineers Fox, Henderson and Company originated many of the modular building techniques that are in use today. Ready-made cast-iron beams were tested at ground level, then hoisted into place by crane.

Electricity enters here

Light is produced between electrodes when electric current is switched on

Tube is connected to electricity supply at each end

Electrode

Partial vacuum

Geissler vacuum tube

1854•
VACUUM TUBE
Julius Plücker and Heinrich Geissler

German physicist Julius Plücker devised the cathode-ray tube on which all television tubes are based. Glassblower Heinrich Geissler made the tubes for Plücker's experiments and sucked the air out of them with a vacuum pump of his own design.

TRAVEL & CONQUEST

1852•
AIRSHIP
Henri Giffard

A balloon floats freely wherever the wind takes it; airships, by contrast, have some sort of power. French inventor Henri Giffard built the first working life-size airship. The craft's steam engine drove it at only 10 kph (6 mph) in still air, but it picked up speed with the wind behind it.

French airship, 1883

•1853 GLIDER *George Cayley*

English flying pioneer George Cayley experimented with kites for many years before building a glider big enough to carry a pilot in free flight. Too old to attempt the flight himself, Cayley ordered his coachman to do it. He glided safely across a valley in uncontrolled flight, but on landing, the reluctant pilot immediately left his job so as not to have to fly again. *See* HANG GLIDER 1891.

Cayley's glider

WORLD EVENTS

1850–1854

•1850 The population of the world is about 1,200 million.

•1851 In London the world's first trade fair, the Great Exhibition, celebrates the "Industry of All Nations".

•1851 In China, the Taiping radicals begin a series of

The Great Exhibition

revolts against the Ch'ing dynasty (ruling family).

•1853 English physician John Snow traces an outbreak of cholera to a polluted well in London's Soho district, and thus establishes the modern science of epidemiology (the

study and control of the spread of infectious disease).

•1854 Threatened by the USA, Japanese leaders sign a treaty in which their nation agrees to start trading with foreigners. The treaty ends centuries of isolation.

Florence Nightingale

•1854 Four European nations fight Russia in the Crimean War. Both sides lose far more soldiers from disease than from wounds, and nurses Florence Nightingale and Mary Seacole become famous for their pioneering care of the sick troops.

1855

1855	1856	1857	1858

•1855 PRINTING TELEGRAPH *David Hughes*

Early coded telegraph messages required an expert hand to tap them out and a perceptive ear to decode them. In 1855, American music teacher, David Hughes streamlined the system with his printing telegraph. The operator tapped in a message on a piano-like keyboard. This sent pulses down the wire to an identical receiving instrument. There, the pulses pressed raised characters against a ribbon of paper to print the message in words.

Telegraph printer was powered by a clockwork mechanism with a driving weight

David Hughes' teleprinter

•1858 PUNCHED PAPER TAPE *Charles Wheatstone*

In common with David Hughes (left), Charles Wheatstone tried to improve the electric telegraph. To speed up the process of sending messages, Wheatstone created a machine that recorded the dots and dashes of Morse code as holes in paper tape. The operator could key in the message slowly, then run the tape through a machine to send it down the wire at high speed.

Punched paper tape machine, 1858

Paper tape on a reel

Keys

Hole punch

A simple coded message is recorded as holes punched on the paper tape.

Flame comes out here

•1855 CAN OPENER *Robert Yeates*

In the 1850s, a number of inventors devised tools that made the job of opening the first cans easier, without the need for a hammer and chisel. Englishman Robert Yeates patented a claw-shaped opener in 1855. The famous bull's head became widespread in the USA a decade later when it was provided free with tinned beef. *See* CANNED FOOD **1811**.

Turning this ring covers or opens a hole in the Bunsen's base and regulates the air supply.

Bunsen burner

Handle

Bull's head

Bull's head can opener

Gas supply flows through this pipe to burner

Blade

Rechargeable electrodes of lead and lead oxide in sulphuric acid

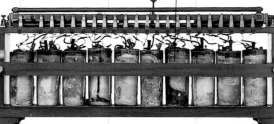

Accumulator battery

Muslin dress coloured purple with aniline dye, c.1860

•1855 BUNSEN BURNER *Robert Bunsen*

Coal gas gives a feeble flame when it burns, but mixing air with the gas produces a much hotter flame. German chemist Robert Bunsen took advantage of this in creating his Bunsen burner – a small laboratory gas burner, with a controllable flame used for scientific experiments.

•1856 ANILINE DYES *William Perkin*

Dyers used natural pigments up until 1856 when an English chemist produced the first synthetic dyes by accident. In his home laboratory, William Perkin was trying to make the drug quinine from the chemical aniline. He produced only a black sludge, but boiling it with water gave a brilliant purple-coloured solution – a chemical dye that would make him a rich man.

•1859 ACCUMULATOR BATTERY *Gaston Planté*

Volta's battery (*see* **1800**) was an expendable cell: its zinc plates dissolved as it was used. In 1859, Frenchman Gaston Planté made the first rechargeable cell using two pieces of lead foil. Separating them with a piece of flannel cut from his wife's petticoat, he rolled the foil and immersed it in acid. He charged (stored power in) the cell by connecting it to electricity.

The Bessemer process for making steel

•1856 STEEL MANUFACTURE *Henry Bessemer*

Making steel involves melting pig iron and burning off some of the carbon it contains. Steel was a very expensive metal to produce until Englishman Henry Bessemer demonstrated a new steel-making process in 1856. Though others claim to have invented this process, Bessemer was the first to patent it and to this day it is named after him.

Two converters

Converter in horizontal position so molten iron can be added

Handle to rotate converter

Converter in upright position to receive blast of air

Blast of air is injected here

Otto's internal combustion engine

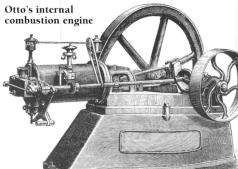

•1859 INTERNAL COMBUSTION ENGINE *Étienne Lenoir*

The engines that power most land vehicles today are combustion engines: tiny explosions in their cylinders drive the pistons back and forth. Frenchman Étienne Lenoir built the first practical one in 1859. Powered by a mixture of gas and air, it was too costly to run. Only in 1878, when German Nikolaus August Otto built a better gas combustion engine, did it begin to compete with steam. *See* PETROL ENGINE **1884**.

•**1855** Scottish missionary-explorer David Livingstone is the first European to see the huge Victoria Falls on Africa's River Zambezi. Inspired by his reports, other Europeans rush to explore and exploit the continent's natural resources.

Livingstone's expedition to Africa

•**1856** The fossilized remains of a prehistoric human are found in the Neander Valley, Germany. The sub-species is later named Neanderthals.
•**1856** French writer Gustave Flaubert finishes his book *Madame Bovary*, but it is banned as indecent before it can go on sale. Once the ban is lifted sales of the book boom.

•**1857** James Murray begins the *Oxford English Dictionary*. By 1884, he has only got as far as "Ant", and he dies in 1915, 13 years before the huge dictionary is completed.
•**1857** The collapse of an insurance company causes panic in the New York Stock Market, leading to a depression in which nearly 5,000 American businesses go bankrupt.
•**1850s** Increasing European settlement in North America threatens Native American land.

Native Americans defend their land

1860

1861   1862   1864

•1861 COLOUR PHOTOGRAPH
James C. Maxwell
Scottish physicist James Clerk Maxwell demonstrated three-colour photography. He photographed a tartan ribbon (shown above) three times using troughs of coloured water as filters. Projecting the processed images together through the same filters reconstructed the colours on a screen. Though Maxwell's process worked, it wasn't practical for everyday photography.
See AUTOCHROME PHOTOGRAPHY **1903**.

c.1861 POSTCARD *Obscure*
The precise origins of the postcard are uncertain. American stationer Hyman L. Lipman may have printed the first postcards in 1861, after buying the copyright to them from the inventor John P. Charlton. Other sources state that the postcard was first invented in Austria some eight years later. Wherever they originated, postcards were in widespread circulation by the 1870s. Pre-stamped postcards were so popular when they first went on sale in Britain that police were called to control the crowds queuing to buy them.

British postcards, 1870

•1860 LINOLEUM *Frederick Walton*
English inventor Frederick Walton devised linoleum as a floor covering that would be cheaper than carpet, but more hard-wearing than painted canvas. Walton coated jute (sack-cloth) with a mixture of ground cork, resin, gum, colouring material, and solidified linseed oil.

Advertisement for linoleum

•1862 PASTEURIZATION
Louis Pasteur
Fresh milk soured so quickly that people could only drink it if it came from somewhere close by. In 1862, French chemist Louis Pasteur invented a heating process to kill off the bacteria in milk. Pasteur demonstrated that bacterial action sours milk; raising its temperature to 70°C (158°F) not only kept the milk fresh for longer, but also stopped it from carrying the deadly diseases tuberculosis and brucellosis.

Louis Pasteur in his laboratory

1860–1870 MACHINE-MADE SPIRAL DRILL BIT
Various
All drill bits were spoon- or gouge-like until the invention of the spiral bit (twist drill). These made much faster rates of drilling possible. They first became common with the development of machines to manufacture them in the 1860s.

•1861 PLASTICS *Various*
British chemist Alexander Parkes made a crude plastic, "Parkesine", from cotton wool and mothballs. Soaking the cotton wool in nitric acid made nitrocellulose, and adding camphor (mothballs) turned it into a substance that could be moulded and shaped. American John Wesley Hyatt later improved Parkes' invention and called it celluloid.

Parkesine hair slide

•1862 MILKING MACHINE *L.O. Colvin*
The time-consuming task of milking cows got a little quicker in 1860, when an American engineer invented an early form of milking machine to do the job. Hoses linked rubber cups on the cow's teats to an enclosed chamber, to which a bellows was attached. Pumping on the bellows milked the cow.

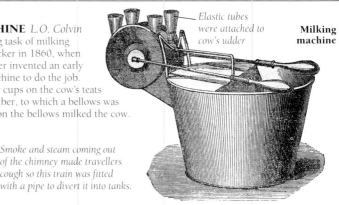

Elastic tubes were attached to cow's udder

Milking machine

Water tank

Funnel

Smoke and steam coming out of the chimney made travellers cough so this train was fitted with a pipe to divert it into tanks.

METROPOLITAN 23 RAILWAY.

•1863 UNDERGROUND RAILWAY *London*
London's expectations for the world's first underground railway were low. One newspaper described it as "an insult to common sense to suppose that people...would ever prefer...to be driven amid palpable darkness through the foul subsoil of London". It opened in 1863, and Londoners soon flocked on to the train, referring to it affectionately as the "drain". The first underground trains were operated by steam locomotives; deep tunnel trains only became possible in 1890 with the introduction of electric locomotives.

London Metropolitan Railway steam locomotive, 1866

1860–1864

•**1860** At war with Japanese-occupied China, Russia captures territory on the Pacific coast of Siberia, and founds the town of Vladivostok.

•**1861** Civil war begins in the USA when the southern states leave the union over the issues of slavery, taxation, and interference in state affairs. War rages for four years.

US Civil War

•**1861** Italy is united as a single kingdom, bringing together the many feuding city-states.

•**1861** After crossing Australia from south to north, white explorers Robert O'Hara Burke and William Wills die on their return journey, despite help from Aboriginal Australians.

Red Cross flag

•**1862** The Civil War in the USA cuts off the supplies of cotton on which British spinning and weaving mills depend, and many mills close.

•**1862** France takes over southern Vietnam, starting a process of colonization that continues for 30 years. French influence in the region ends only in the 1950s.

•**1864** Lack of care for war victims provokes Jean Henri Dunant of Switzerland to call for an international volunteer aid organization – the Red Cross is formed.

1865

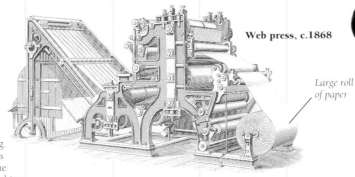

Web press, c.1868

Large roll of paper

US stapler, c.1880

Paper to be stapled inserted here

•1865 WEB PRINTING PRESS *Various*

Steam power had made printing much quicker by the 1860s, but feeding sheets of paper into the presses limited their speed. The problem was solved by feeding paper in a web – from a roll. The first newspaper to be printed like this was the *Philadelphia Enquirer*, though its presses cut sheets from the roll before printing. Three years later the London *Times* installed a rotary press in which the web passed uncut through the machine.

Spray

Barbed wire, 1867

•1865 ANTISEPTIC SURGERY *Joseph Lister*

Joseph Lister was the first to put antiseptic principles into practice in surgery although they had been applied to other areas of medicine. He soaked dressings in carbolic acid to kill germs, and sprayed it around the operating theatre. His ideas laid the foundations for modern surgical safety.

Antiseptic carbolic steam spray, 1875

Steam generator

Carbolic acid reservoir

•1865 RIVETING MACHINE *William Fairbairn*

To join large metal sheets, boiler-makers used thousands of rivets (metal plugs). These were heated and applied by hand. Prolific Scottish engineer and inventor William Fairbairn introduced a steam-powered riveting machine to make this task quicker around 1865.

1867–1868 BARBED WIRE *Various*

Barbed wire was first patented around 1867, but it wasn't until 1874, when a US farmer, Joseph F. Glidden, built the first wire-making machine, that its mass-production became practical. Barbed wire doomed the livelihood of the American cowboy. Fenced fields meant the end of free-ranging cattle and the end of the cattle drive.

•1868 STAPLER *C.H. Gould*

A British patent for a stapler was issued in 1868. The first staples fastened the soles and uppers of shoes. Stapling of paper began in the printing industry in the 1890s, and spread to the office where staples slowly replaced pins and clips.

•1868 AIR-POWERED DENTAL DRILL *George Green*

American mechanic George Green shortened the agony of dental patients in 1868 with his air-powered drill. The dentist pumped a foot bellows, and the air flowed along a hose to power the drill, which was small enough to hold in one hand.

•1867 REINFORCED CONCRETE *Joseph Monier*

The ancestor of today's soaring concrete bridges was a flowerpot! French gardener Joseph Monier began making flowerpots using concrete and wire netting in 1867 and found that the wire reinforcement gave the concrete enough strength to resist tension. *See* **CONCRETE BRIDGE 1894.**

•1866 DRY-CELL BATTERY *Georges Leclanché*

French railway engineer Leclanché produced the forerunner of today's handy torch batteries in 1867. His cell was powerful, simple, and worked well with occasional use over long periods. These qualities made it the ideal cell for the emerging telegraph networks.

Carbon rod

Terminal

•1868 GEYSER *Benjamin W. Maughan*

Piped hot water was a luxury, until inventor Benjamin Waddy Maughan devised a gas water heater to warm bathwater. Called a geyser, its advantage was that it delivered hot water on demand – there was no waiting while the water heated up. His early heaters were at best, temperamental and at worst, explosive, and the careless bather risked singed hair.

1865–1867 DYNAMITE *Alfred Nobel*

Swedish explosives maker Alfred Nobel made safe the powerful, yet unstable, explosive nitroglycerine (*see* **1846**) by mixing it with kieselguhr, a kind of earth. This made a grey paste which was not detonated by shock. Mining and military engineers soon began to use the new explosive.

•1865 DETONATOR *Alfred Nobel*

A stick of dynamite is safe to transport; even when lit with a flame, it does not explode. To trigger a blast from it, Alfred Nobel also invented a detonator. Nobel's detonator, made of mercury fulminate, exploded violently when lit, and this initial explosion set off the much more powerful dynamite.

Nobel detonator

Fuse

Rock surround

Detonator of mercury fulminate

Explosive charge

Zinc rod

Electrolyte of ammonium chloride solution

Leclanché cell

•1866 TORPEDO *Robert Whitehead*

Naval warfare, already made more deadly by mines and better guns, received another boost in 1866 with the invention of the self-propelled torpedo. A propeller driven by compressed air powered it towards the target, and pressure sensors operated small fins to maintain its depth. It could carry 8.2 kg (18 lb) of explosives.

•1869 AIR BRAKES *George Westinghouse*

As railway systems grew, accidents were often caused by trains with faulty brakes. In 1869, an American engineer devised a fail-safe air brake system. It relied on a vacuum tube running the length of the train. Sucking air from the tube released the brakes. To apply them, the driver opened a valve, letting air into the tube.

Whitehead torpedo

•**1865** English author Lewis Carroll (whose real name was Charles Dodgson) writes *Alice's Adventures in Wonderland* to amuse Alice Liddell, the daughter of a friend.
•**1865** In the USA, Confederate forces (southern states) surrender to the Union army (northern), ending the damaging civil war and eventually ending slavery.
•**1866** Austrian monk Gregor Mendel publishes the first research in genetics. He helps explain how plants and animals pass on their characteristics to their offspring.

Lewis Carroll's Alice

•**1867** Prospectors find diamonds in South Africa. This discovery, and that of gold 20 years later, start industrial development of the country.
•**1868** Deals with foreigners weaken Japan's shogun rulers, and the Japanese imperial family once more takes power. Emperor Meiji, aged 16, rules the country.

•**1869** In Egypt, the Suez Canal opens, allowing ships to sail through the strip of land linking the Red Sea and the Mediterranean and cutting the distance between Europe and India.
•**1869** The National Woman Suffrage Association is established in the USA to campaign for voting and property rights for women.

Building the Suez Canal

1870–1939 Electric power and the modern world

In 1870, ELECTRICITY was no longer a toy. A century earlier, things had been different: the only value of electricity then was to amuse party guests. Rubbing silk on amber, they laughed at the spectacular static electric sparks.

Electricity had grown up by 1870, but it was not yet a tool. Scientists had created basic electrical machines, such as the dynamo and the electric motor, but these devices were still just laboratory novelties. The most widespread use of electricity was in sending messages. A communications cable spanned the Atlantic – but it crackled with the dots and dashes of Morse code, not speech. Even electric lighting was a clumsy novelty. Electric lamps produced light from an alarming and noisy spark that leaped between two carbon rods. These "arc lamps" lit streets and railway stations, but were far too bright for the home.

Light for the home

House and office lighting did not become practical until 1879, when the incandescent bulb that we use today was perfected. The bulb itself was easy to make: every experimenter knew that a thin wire filament glowed brightly when a high volume of electricity passed through it. The problem lay in making the bulb last, because the glowing wire quickly burned through. The search for a filament that would not burn was long and frustrating. Inventor Thomas Edison experimented with many different materials. "I've tried everything," he said at one point, "I have not failed. I've just found 10,000 ways that won't work." Finally, his researchers struck lucky – with carbonized sewing thread. Inside the glass globe, the thread of carbon shone for two days before it burned out.

ELECTRIC LIGHT
The first electric light bulbs were called filament or incandescent bulbs, because of the way they worked. Electricity flowed through a thin piece of carbon with high resistance – the filament. This became so hot that it glowed white, or incandesced. If the filament glowed in air, oxygen in the air would combine with it and quickly burn it away. So air was sucked out of the bulb to create a vacuum around the filament.

Edison's screw-in bulb

Electric lighting at Chesterfield, England, in 1882

THE CHANGING WORLD: 1870–1939

Charles Lindbergh in 1927 after his Atlantic flight

MOTOR CAR
When the motor car was invented in 1885, only the very rich could afford to buy them. But when Henry Ford started mass-producing the Model T in 1908, suddenly a car was within many more people's reach. By 1930, over 15 million Model Ts had been sold in the USA. New roads had to be built to cater for the demand, and making cars became a boom industry.

STEEL STRENGTH
Within 20 years of the invention of a way of making cheap steel, people began to realize its potential for building. The Brooklyn Bridge, which opened in 1883 in the USA, was the world's first large steel-wire suspension bridge. Steel was also widely adopted for making machines and building railways.

1914 Model T Ford

POWERED FLIGHT
When Charles Lindbergh first flew across the Atlantic in 1927, he fulfilled the dreams of many thousands before him. People were quick to accept the new form of transport, and the demand for faster travel pushed inventors to experiment with new designs.

COMMUNICATION BY WIRE…
The advantages, both personal and professional, of being able to talk to people hundreds of miles away are endless. The telephone, invented in 1876, gradually became a necessity.

Electric light bulbs soon lit the cities of Europe and America and the word "electric" came to stand for "modern". Businesses everywhere wanted the new electric light for their offices, shops, and signs. People began travelling to work by electricity: by the 1880s the sparking of electric trams competed with the clatter of horses' hooves on the cobbled city streets. The telephone, invented in 1876, gave a further boost to the electric age, as electricity carried conversations for hundreds of miles.

Faster communication

When Brazilian Emperor Pedro II first used a telephone in 1876, he dropped the instrument exclaiming "It talks!". But as phones became more common and more familiar, they changed everyone's sense of distance and separation. Telephones brought people together just as evolving transport systems were making it easier for them to move farther apart.

The arrival of radio in 1906 seemed to shrink distances once again, but in a subtly different way. Telephones provided one-to-one communication, but radio made possible "broad" casting. By transmitting the same message to a huge group of listeners, radio drew nations together, giving them a shared sense of community and purpose.

Electricity's slow advance

Despite these exciting advances, it was a long time before electricity arrived in people's homes. As electricity companies expanded their webs of cables, power lines soon reached town houses, but almost the only use of electricity was for lighting. Electric heaters, cookers, and the many other appliances we use today became common only in the 20th century. People in country areas had to rely on oil lamps and candles for much longer before they were connected to the network. Even when power lines passed the door, only wealthy families could afford to install cables and pay for the power. Of all the people born the year light bulbs were invented, just one in eight celebrated their 40th birthday in a home lit by electricity.

THE PROCESS OF INVENTION

THE RISE OF THE RESEARCH LAB...

Edison in his laboratory, 1889

American Thomas Edison was among the first to realize that, as technology became more complicated, no one inventor could master all the skills needed to perfect and market an invention. He assembled a team of around 70 skilled scientists, engineers, and mechanics and established the first research laboratory in Menlo Park, New Jersey. There, his employees had access to a machine shop, a science reference library, and workshops for electrical and mechanical devices. Edison's venture was so successful that others soon followed his example. In 1902, the American Du Pont Corporation opened a similar research facility, which developed Nylon, Teflon, and Kevlar plastics. Today, research and development (R & D) laboratories are necessary for any large industrial corporation.

...BUT STILL ROOM FOR THE LONE INVENTOR

Many experts claim that most inventions are determined by economic and technological conditions and that colourful tales of absent-minded but brilliant lone inventors are little more than fiction. Yet individuals continued to influence the course of technology long after R & D laboratories had begun. Perhaps the most inspiring examples of individual effort and soaring achievement were the Wright brothers. In 1903, Wilbur and Orville made the first powered flights in a heavier-than-air flying machine. They were not experts and they did not rely on heavy financial backing – they simply had enough insight, energy, and creativity to take to the air and to control their craft in flight. They literally flew in the face of expert opinion.

The first powered flight, by Orville and Wilbur Wright in 1903

...WIRELESS COMMUNICATION

By the 1920s, many radio transmitters had been built and radio was within the reach of households in Europe and the USA. Radio could entertain and inform people in their own homes.

THE OFFICE

The invention of office equipment, such as typewriters, changed the way people worked. These new, often low-paid desk jobs were filled mainly by women.

MEDICAL ADVANCES

Between the end of the 19th century and the start of World War II, medicine changed drastically. The invention of vaccines and antibiotics for treating once-fatal diseases prolonged life. The widespread use of X-rays made it easier for doctors to diagnose illness.

THE DISPOSABLE ERA

Today, we happily discard almost anything, knowing we can simply buy another. But until the beginning of the 20th century, we would have been more likely to have belongings repaired. The throw-away age began with the invention of disposable razor blades in 1901.

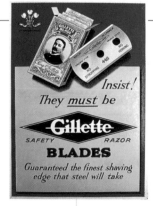

ARTIFICIAL MATERIALS

The invention of Bakelite in 1909 gave manufacturers a versatile new raw material. Plastics come in a vast range of different forms and have the advantage of being tough and non-toxic. By 1940, plastics were appearing in many households, and stockings of nylon were replacing silk.

Bakelite hair dryer

1870

1870	1871	1872	1873	1874

COUNTING & COMMUNICATION

Box of dry plates, c.1890

•1871 PHOTOGRAPHIC DRY PLATES *Richard Leach Maddox*

Before the 1870s, photographers did not use film: they had to coat glass plates with a syrupy goo in a darkroom, then take and process the photograph before the coating dried. Englishman Richard Leach Maddox eliminated this complicated routine when he invented dry gelatin plates. These were factory-made plates coated with a light-sensitive gelatin layer. Maddox's idea popularized photography, but the age of the snapshot began with Hannibal Goodwin's 1887 invention of flexible film and George Eastman's Kodak camera of 1888.

•1873 TYPEWRITER *Christopher Latham Sholes*

Individual writing machines were patented as early as 1714, but the first typewriters to be produced in quantity came from the Remington Company in the 1870s. They were developed by American, Christopher Latham Sholes. He and various partners spent years improving the machine, especially the keyboard. Finding that typists often jammed the keys, they moved the most common letters to positions that were harder to reach. This gave us the QWERTYUIOP arrangement of keys on the top line that is still in use today. He finished the machine in 1873, and Remington put it on the market in 1874.

Sholes and Glidden for Remington typewriter, 1873

Keys

This arrangement of keys is still used today on modern computers, even though their keys cannot jam.

Weight to counterbalance carriage return above

Typewriters like this were often operated by women, at a lower rate of pay than that earned by the clerks they replaced.

DAILY LIFE & HEALTH

Packets of chewing gum, c.1900

1872• CHEWING GUM *Thomas Adams*

The first person to make sticks of chewing gum from the plant sap, chicle, was an American photographer. He was trying to use up a surplus of chicle he had bought. He knew that Native Americans chewed it, so he added liquorice flavour, called it Black Jack, and put it on sale.

•1871 MARGARINE *H. Mège-Mouriès*

Synthetic butter, now called margarine, was first developed in the 1870s. The French chemist's first attempt, made by mixing beef suet with milk, water, and chopped cow's udder, apparently tasted disgusting.

Margarine advertisement, c.1880

AGRICULTURE & INDUSTRY

Later wind tunnels were big enough to test full-size planes.

TRAVEL & CONQUEST

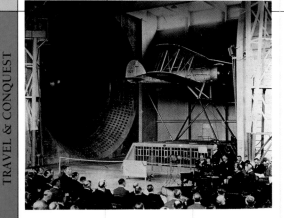

•1871 WIND TUNNEL *Francis Herbert Wenham*

To test an aircraft's flying ability, its designers blow air across a scale model fixed inside a long tube called a wind tunnel. Wind tunnels were used for testing aircraft before the first powered flight. The earliest one was created by Englishman Francis Herbert Wenham in 1871. Driven by a steam engine, the 3-m (10-ft) long tunnel simulated air speeds of up to 65 kph (40 mph).

Plane being tested in a wind tunnel, c.1927

•1872 MONORAIL *Pennsylvania, USA*

In 1872, the world's first permanent powered monorail railway (with a single rail) opened on a route linking Bradford and Derrick City, Pennsylvania. The monorail made little progress until the 1960s. In 1959, a monorail opened in Disneyland, California, USA and this reminded transportation designers of the possibilities of this form of transport. Today, monorail systems have proved more costly than conventional railways, and are less common.

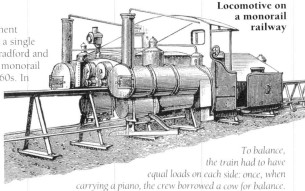

Locomotive on a monorail railway

To balance, the train had to have equal loads on each side: once, when carrying a piano, the crew borrowed a cow for balance.

WORLD EVENTS

1870–1874

•1870 Russian Dmitri Mendeleev arranges all the chemical elements according to their weight in his periodic table, leaving gaps for later discoveries to be added.

•1870 For the first time, American voters elect African Americans to represent them in the Senate.

Terracotta vase found at Troy

•1870 Using clues from Homer's *Illiad*, German archaeologist Heinrich Schliemann discovers the ruins of the ancient city of Troy in Turkey.

•1873 A critic mocks the unfinished appearance of French painter Claude Monet's *Impression: Sunrise*, but artists in Monet's circle like the impressionist label, and adopt it to describe an exhibition of their work.

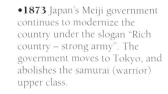

A Japanese samurai (warrior)

•1873 Japan's Meiji government continues to modernize the country under the slogan "Rich country – strong army". The government moves to Tokyo, and abolishes the samurai (warrior) upper class.

1875

1876•
TELEPHONE *Alexander Graham Bell*
While searching for a way to send several simultaneous telegraph messages along a single wire, Alexander Graham Bell invented the telephone. The first words he spoke on it were heard after he spilled battery acid on his trousers. He urgently shouted for help from his assistant – "... come here, I want you!" – who heard the words coming from the new machine they had made.

Hughes' first microphone, 1878

Two Bell telephones, 1876

1878•
MICROPHONE *David Hughes*
American David Hughes first coined the word microphone, even though Bell's telephone had used a similar device. Hughes discovered that loose electrical contacts are very sensitive to vibrations, such as sound. He made a crude microphone to demonstrate how it could change sound into electric current.

•1879
CASH REGISTER *James Ritty*
Bar owner James Ritty of Dayton, Ohio, USA invented the cash register to stop staff from pilfering money. On an Atlantic liner, he saw a machine that counted the turns made by the propellers. He made a cash till that operated in a similar way and patented it. His first till had a dial, but this was soon replaced with pop-up hands to show the amount of sale.

Replica of 1879 Ritty cash register

Brass drum was wrapped with tinfoil

A horn was originally attached to this mouthpiece.

Edison's phonograph

•1877 PHONOGRAPH RECORD PLAYER *Thomas Edison*
Thomas Edison first recorded sound on a strip of tinfoil wrapped around a moving drum or cylinder. When he shouted "Halloo" this vibrated a membrane, and a needle fixed to it scratched a wavy groove around the drum. To his delight, when he turned the drum again the needle in the groove played a faint "Aaoo".

1879•
INCANDESCENT ELECTRIC LAMP *Thomas Edison*
The principle of the light bulb was known long before a successful one was created. The imperfect vacuum in early bulbs meant that the filaments quickly burned in the remaining air. Many people, including US inventor Thomas Edison and British inventor Joseph Swan, searched for a practical solution. In 1879, using a new air pump, Edison produced a commercially viable, high resistance carbon filament lamp.

Partial vacuum

Carbon filament

Edison's lamp

•1875 GELIGNITE *Alfred Nobel*
Alfred Nobel became rich by inventing explosive gelignite. He made it from two other explosives: guncotton (nitrocellulose) and nitroglycerine. The resulting stiff jelly was safer to handle than pure liquid nitroglycerine, yet had almost the same explosive effect. Perhaps concerned about the destructive power of his inventions, Nobel left much of his fortune for the prize that bears his name. The Nobel Prize is awarded annually for outstanding achievement in physics, chemistry, medicine, literature, and peace.

A "pantograph" collects the electric current for the driving motors from an overhead power line.

Patent model of a paper bag machine, 1879

•1879 PAPER BAG MACHINE *Margaret Knight*
The machine manufacture of square-bottomed paper sacks (like the ones used for groceries) was pioneered by the American inventor Margaret Knight. She was dubbed a "woman Edison" by her local newspaper.

Electric train, England, 1904

NORTH EASTERN

1879•
ELECTRIC TRAIN *Germany*
The first demonstration that electric trains were practical took place at a Berlin industrial exhibition in 1879, where a small train buzzed around an oval track. In 1880, a French laundry company began using electric trains to collect linen sheets from the meadows where they were spread to bleach (a steam train would have spread soot). Electric trains were faster, cleaner, and quieter than steam locomotives and slowly replaced them.

•**1875** American author Mark Twain writes *Tom Sawyer*.
•**1876** Greyhound racing with a mechanical hare begins in England on an experimental basis.
•**1877** The myth of Martian people begins when channels marked as *canali* on an Italian map of the planet are mistranslated as "canals".

Mark Twain

•**1877** In Mexico, General Porfirio Diaz becomes President. His administration ends war and banditry and brings stability, prosperity, and peace to the country.
•**1877** White Americans in San Francisco riot against competition for jobs from Chinese labourers, leading to tighter controls on immigration.

•**1878** Aletta Jacobs, the first woman doctor in the Netherlands, opens the world's first birth control clinic.
•**1878** Nils Nordenskjöld of Sweden opens the Northeast Passage by sailing directly from the Atlantic to the Pacific along the north coast of Europe and Asia.
•**1879** Zulu warriors in the Transvaal (now South Africa) defeat and humiliate the British army at Isandhlwana in their battle for control of the region, but the British eventually succeed in imposing European rule.

Nordenskjöld's ship *The Vega*

1880

1880	1881	1882	1883

COUNTING & COMMUNICATION

•1880
SEISMOGRAPH *John Milne*
A seismograph, or earthquake detector, amplifies and records small earth movements and helps scientists to assess the location and intensity of earthquakes. A simple instrument that could indicate only the direction of an earthquake was made in ancient China as long ago as AD 132, but modern seismographs are based on the 1880 work of British scientist John Milne.

•1881 STEREOPHONY *Clement Ader*
Frenchman Clement Ader patented stereophonic sound in Germany in 1881. He used it to broadcast theatre performances to telephone subscribers, who held a telephone earpiece to each ear. Stereo radio broadcasts began in 1925 and stereo records followed five years later.

•1884
LINOTYPE *Ottmar Mergenthaler*
Until 1884, printers had to assemble the text of books and newspapers by picking out individual lead letters from a box. The linotype machine enabled operators to type the text on a keyboard. The machine assembled moulds of the letters in the right order, then poured in molten lead to form the text line by line.

•1884
FOUNTAIN PEN
Lewis Edson Waterman
American insurance salesman Lewis Edson Waterman was about to sign an important document when his pen emptied itself on to the paper. He was so furious that in 1884 he invented the first fountain pen with a regulated ink supply. Earlier pens with built-in ink holders had plungers that had to be pushed from time to time to keep the ink flowing freely.

Fountain pen

DAILY LIFE & HEALTH

1880–1881
GAS FIRE *Sigismund Leoni*
Following Bunsen's experiments with air and gas (*see* **1855**), London engineer Leoni was among the first to make successful gas fires for domestic use. He patented a gas burner, which had tufts of asbestos in its heatproof fireclay. The tufts retained heat and glowed red hot to warm a room.

Electric arc generated by two carbon rods

Heavy cast-iron base to smooth fabrics

Connection for electric flex

Electric iron, c.1885

Turbine blades rotate, and spin armature to generate power

Electromagnet

Steam flows over turbine blades

Armature

1882•
ELECTRIC IRON *Henry W. Seely*
Electric irons were one of the first home electrical appliances: Henry W. Seely of New York introduced them in 1882. The iron was powered by an electric arc and when in use it sputtered and hissed in an alarming way.

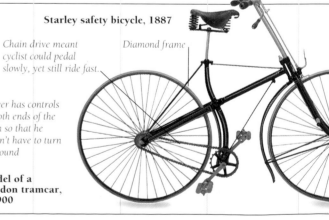

Parson's steam turbine generator, 1884

AGRICULTURE & INDUSTRY

•1881 MUNICIPAL HYDROELECTRIC POWER STATION *England*
The world's first municipal hydroelectric power station used water rushing through turbines installed in an old leather mill in Godalming, England, to generate electricity. The power plant provided street lighting and supplied private homes. Most early power stations, though, used steam to spin the generators. The first large hydroelectric power plant opened in Deptford, south London, in 1889.

Water rushes through turbines, driving dynamos in the powerhouse above.

Hydroelectric power station

•1884
STEAM TURBINE *Charles Parsons*
In 1884, English engineer Charles Parsons revolutionized electric power supply with the invention of his steam turbine. It spun at an astonishing speed of 18,000 revolutions per minute and showed that powerful rotation could be created from steam pressure without a piston. It soon replaced the steam engine in electric generators.

•1884
PETROL ENGINE *Gottlieb Daimler*
The breakthrough in making the internal combustion engine into a practical source of power for road vehicles came from Germany. There, Gottlieb Daimler made the first high-speed, light-weight petrol engines. *See* **INTERNAL COMBUSTION ENGINE 1859**.

TRAVEL & CONQUEST

1881•
TRAMCAR *Werner von Siemens*
German engineer Werner von Siemens built the first electric tramline. His tramline supplied electricity directly to the tramcar motor via its metal wheels. However, pedestrians and horses that trod on the rails were alarmed by the electric shocks they received so this style of tramline did not last long. Americans Leo Daft and Charles J. van Depoele perfected the supply of power from overhead cables, and from 1889, electric tramcars, or trams, rapidly replaced horse-drawn vehicles.

These wires collect electricity from overhead cables to power the tram.

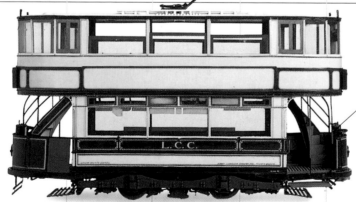

Driver has controls at both ends of the tram so that he doesn't have to turn it around

Model of a London tramcar, c.1900

Starley safety bicycle, 1887

Chain drive meant cyclist could pedal slowly, yet still ride fast.

Diamond frame

WORLD EVENTS

1880–1884

•**1880** French physician Charles Laveran shows that a parasite in the blood causes the deadly disease malaria. People used to think "bad air" was to blame.
•**1881** Russian Czar Alexander III blames Jews for his father's murder and encourages their persecution. Over the next 25 years there is a series of pogroms – riots killing Jews and destroying their property.
•**1881** In what is now South Africa, the Boers (Dutch) defeat the British in a war over territory.

First Boer war

•**1881** Outlaw and 21-times murderer Billy the Kid, aged 21, is shot dead in New Mexico. Within months he is a popular US hero.
•**1883** The volcanic island of Krakatoa erupts in Indonesia, killing 36,000 people. The explosion is so loud that people 4,800 km (3,000 miles) away hear it.

Krakatoa erupts

•**1883** The Brooklyn Bridge is finished in New York, and the first skyscraper (10 floors) appears on the skyline of Chicago.
•**1884** The War of the Pacific, between Peru, Bolivia, and Chile, ends with victory for Chile. As a result, Peru and Bolivia both lose valuable territories.

1885

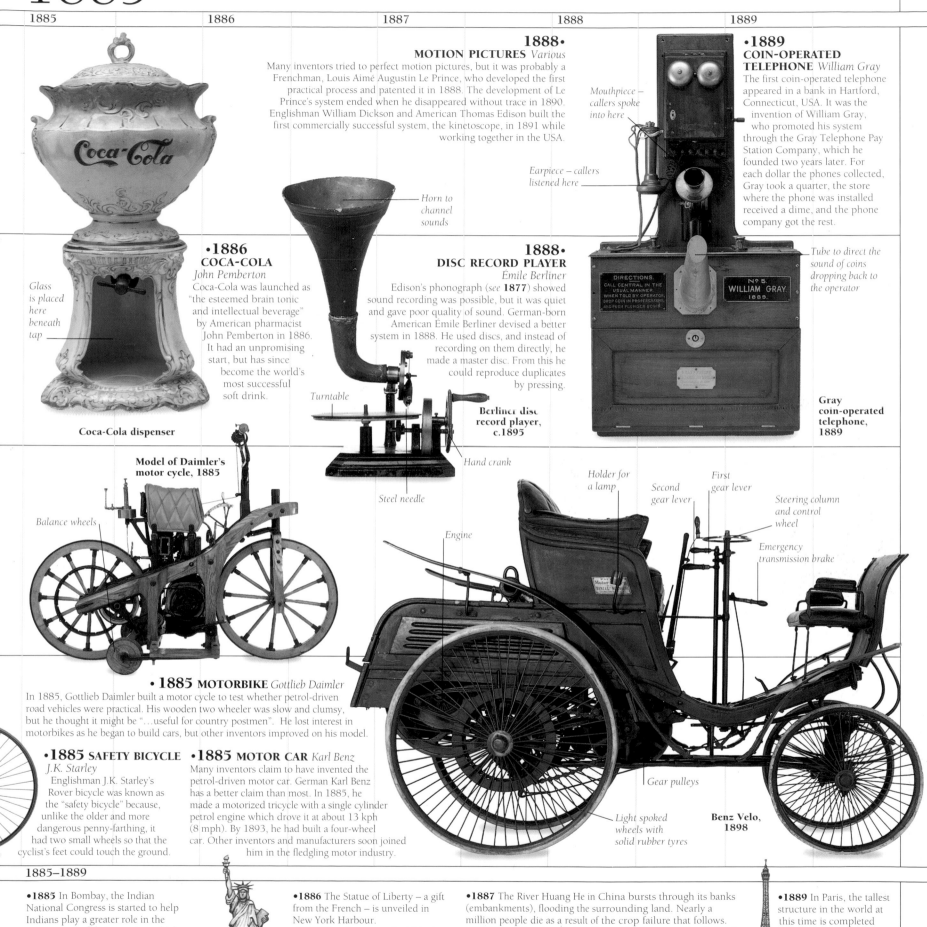

•1888
MOTION PICTURES *Various*
Many inventors tried to perfect motion pictures, but it was probably a Frenchman, Louis Aimé Augustin Le Prince, who developed the first practical process and patented it in 1888. The development of Le Prince's system ended when he disappeared without trace in 1890. Englishman William Dickson and American Thomas Edison built the first commercially successful system, the kinetoscope, in 1891 while working together in the USA.

•1889
COIN-OPERATED TELEPHONE *William Gray*
The first coin-operated telephone appeared in a bank in Hartford, Connecticut, USA. It was the invention of William Gray, who promoted his system through the Gray Telephone Pay Station Company, which he founded two years later. For each dollar the phones collected, Gray took a quarter, the store where the phone was installed received a dime, and the phone company got the rest.

Mouthpiece – callers spoke into here

Earpiece – callers listened here

Horn to channel sounds

•1886
COCA-COLA
John Pemberton
Coca-Cola was launched as "the esteemed brain tonic and intellectual beverage" by American pharmacist John Pemberton in 1886. It had an unpromising start, but has since become the world's most successful soft drink.

Glass is placed here beneath tap

1888•
DISC RECORD PLAYER
Émile Berliner
Edison's phonograph (*see* **1877**) showed sound recording was possible, but it was quiet and gave poor quality of sound. German-born American Émile Berliner devised a better system in 1888. He used discs, and instead of recording on them directly, he made a master disc. From this he could reproduce duplicates by pressing.

Turntable

Tube to direct the sound of coins dropping back to the operator

DIRECTIONS.
CALL CENTRAL IN THE USUAL MANNER.
WHEN TOLD BY OPERATOR, DROP COIN IN PROPER CHANNEL AND PUSH PLUNGER DOWN.

Nº 5.
WILLIAM GRAY.
1889.

Gray coin-operated telephone, 1889

Coca-Cola dispenser

Berliner disc record player, c.1895

Steel needle

Hand crank

Model of Daimler's motor cycle, 1885

Balance wheels

Holder for a lamp

Second gear lever

First gear lever

Steering column and control wheel

Engine

Emergency transmission brake

• 1885 MOTORBIKE *Gottlieb Daimler*
In 1885, Gottlieb Daimler built a motor cycle to test whether petrol-driven road vehicles were practical. His wooden two wheeler was slow and clumsy, but he thought it might be "…useful for country postmen". He lost interest in motorbikes as he began to build cars, but other inventors improved on his model.

•1885 SAFETY BICYCLE
J.K. Starley
Englishman J.K. Starley's Rover bicycle was known as the "safety bicycle" because, unlike the older and more dangerous penny-farthing, it had two small wheels so that the cyclist's feet could touch the ground.

•1885 MOTOR CAR *Karl Benz*
Many inventors claim to have invented the petrol-driven motor car. German Karl Benz has a better claim than most. In 1885, he made a motorized tricycle with a single cylinder petrol engine which drove it at about 13 kph (8 mph). By 1893, he had built a four-wheel car. Other inventors and manufacturers soon joined him in the fledgling motor industry.

Gear pulleys

Benz Velo, 1898

Light spoked wheels with solid rubber tyres

•**1885** In Bombay, the Indian National Congress is started to help Indians play a greater role in the government of their country, which is under British rule.
•**1885** English scientist Francis Galton proves that no two people's fingerprints are identical, and that the pattern remains the same for life.

•**1886** The Statue of Liberty – a gift from the French – is unveiled in New York Harbour.
•**1886** The discovery of gold in the Transvaal (now South Africa) leads to a gold rush.

Statue of Liberty

•**1887** The River Huang He in China bursts through its banks (embankments), flooding the surrounding land. Nearly a million people die as a result of the crop failure that follows.
•**1887** English writer Arthur Conan Doyle creates the fictional detective Sherlock Holmes when he writes *A Study in Scarlet*.
•**1889** The publication of the Japanese constitution is another step forward in the westernization of the country. Elections begin the following year, but only one person in every hundred can vote.

•**1889** In Paris, the tallest structure in the world at this time is completed to celebrate the Paris Exhibition. The tower is named after Gustave Eiffel – its designer.

Eiffel Tower

1890

1890	1891	1892	1893	1894

COUNTING & COMMUNICATION

Light   Fuses

Switches to control the electric hotplates

Wires connecting switchboard to cooker

Iron hotplates

Electric hob

1889–1892
AUTOMATIC TELEPHONE EXCHANGE
Almon Brown Strowger
Early telephone calls were made by cranking a handle and asking the operator for the number. Undertaker Almon Brown Strowger of Kansas City, USA, felt sure that the operator was directing his calls to a rival. To prevent this, he invented the dial telephone and an automatic exchange, which enabled callers to bypass the operator. The first system was installed in 1892 and made possible the rapid growth of the telephone network. Strowger, by the way, was right: the operator was the wife of a rival undertaker.

Reflector

Enormous cylindrical bulbs glowed orange or red when in use. They looked warm but in fact gave out little heat.

Early electric fire with Dowsing bulbs

DAILY LIFE & HEALTH

Electric cooker, c.1900

•1891 ELECTRIC OVEN
Carpenter Electric Company, USA
A few restaurant kitchens cooked on electric ranges as early as 1889, but the first home electric oven was sold in 1891, by the Carpenter Electric Company of St. Paul, Minnesota, USA. However, few households had a power supply, so early sales were slow.

•1891 ELECTRIC KETTLE
Carpenter Electric Company, USA
The first electric kettles boiled slowly and had non-renewable heating elements fixed in the base. They were launched by the Carpenter Electric Company of St. Paul, Minnesota, USA in 1891.

•1892 ELECTRIC FIRE *Rookes Evelyn Bell Crompton and Herbert Dowsing*
Bell Crompton and his partner Dowsing patented the first electric fires in Great Britain in 1892, but they did not sell well. In 1906, Albert Marsh, of Illinois, USA, devised a heatproof alloy of nickel and chrome. Heating elements made from "Nichrome" could glow red hot without snapping. The first efficient fire using Nichrome was produced in 1912.

Electric kettle

From the 1920s onwards, kettles were made with waterproof heating elements inside them, rather than in the base.

Bulb to inflate cuff

AGRICULTURE & INDUSTRY

Tailplane

Canvas or cotton wing supported by willow rods to hold its shape

Willow hoop acts as a shock absorber

•1894
CONCRETE BRIDGE
François Hennebique
French structural engineer François Hennebique was one of the first designers to make use of Monier's invention of reinforced concrete. His bridges at Viggen in Switzerland, built in 1894, and Châterallerault in France, built in 1898, were among the first important reinforced concrete bridges in the world. *See* **REINFORCED CONCRETE 1867**.

TRAVEL & CONQUEST

1891•
HANG GLIDER *Otto Lilienthal*
Despite George Cayley's demonstration of the glider in 1853, human flight still seemed an impossible dream in the 1890s; those who attempted it were nicknamed "tower jumpers". Otto Lilienthal, a German, made a controlled glider – today we call it a hang glider – in around 1891. He built a bat-wing shaped craft from stretched canvas, and made hundreds of flights, rising as high as 350 m (1,150 ft). Lilienthal was killed while flying one of his machines.

Replica of Lilienthal's hang glider of 1895

•1893
AUTOMATIC PISTOL *Germany*
A pistol designed by Hugo Borchardt and made in Berlin in 1893 was the first self-loading, or semi-automatic, pistol. A magazine held eight shots and the gun fired one each time the user pulled the trigger. Spent cartridge cases were automatically ejected. The automatics were used exclusively as anti-personnel weapons, and they brought a new efficiency to violent death.

•1892 DIESEL ENGINE *Rudolph Diesel*
Compressed and heated, fuel oil explodes spontaneously, even without a spark; engines that work on this principle are named after the German engineer Rudolph Diesel, who proposed the idea in 1890. He built his first engine in 1892.

WORLD EVENTS

1890–1894

•1890 The Battle of Wounded Knee – the last major battle between Native Americans and white settlers – breaks out. Around 300 Sioux, including women and children, are slaughtered.

Sioux warrior

•1890
Indian poet Rabindranath Tagore publishes a book of poetry: Manasi (The Mind's Embodiment).
•1891 The German government introduces the world's first compulsory senior citizens' pension scheme. Germans pay into the scheme while they work and draw a pension on reaching 70 years of age.

•1893 Queen Liliuokalani of Hawaii loses her throne in a revolt inspired by the island's American sugar-planters. The USA annexes (takes over) Hawaii five years later.
•1893 New Zealand is the first country to give women the right to vote.

Women voters in New Zealand

•1893 Figures show that US buffalo hunters have reduced the number of buffalo to fewer than 1100. Before European settlers arrived in North America, there were more than 30 million of them.
•1894 British author Rudyard Kipling writes The Jungle Book for children.

1895

•1895 RADIO *Guglielmo Marconi*

After reading the scientific writings of Heinrich Hertz, 20-year-old Italian Guglielmo Marconi invented radio communication. He experimented with a crude transmitter, which used sparks to create radio waves. At first, he sent signals across the room, then he moved the receiver outside, and finally, his brother carried it over the hill, signalling successful reception by firing a gun. Marconi's greatest triumph came in 1901 when he sent a signal across the Atlantic.

Curved reflector

Electromagnetic waves are transmitted from here.

Radio transmitter, 1896

Poulsen's machine used 2 m (7 ft) of wire for each second of speech recorded.

Poulsen telegraphone, 1903

•1898 MAGNETIC SOUND RECORDING *Valdemar Poulsen*

At the end of the 19th century, Danish engineer Valdemar Poulsen invented his telegraphone. It recorded sound by magnetizing piano wire in a pattern of pulses that corresponded to sound waves. Modern tape recorders using the same principle were invented in 1935.

•1895 X-RAYS
Wilhelm Röntgen

In a laboratory in Germany, physicist Wilhelm Röntgen made a remarkable discovery. He found that a piece of paper painted with crystals glowed when he switched on a vacuum tube, and guessed that a ray coming from the tube caused it. The rays, which he called X-rays, even passed through when the tube was covered with metal. Röntgen then found that X-rays could expose photographic plates, and before long, doctors were using X-rays to take photographs of bones in the body.

Sphygmomanometer

•1896 SPHYGMOMANOMETER
Scipione Riva-Rocci

Doctors knew sick patients had weak pulses centuries before Riva-Rocci devised an instrument to read blood pressure. However, the Italian's sphygmomanometer made precise measurement possible. Wrapped around the arm, its hollow cuff cut off the blood supply when inflated. By releasing air, the physician could measure the pressure at which blood flow started again.

Cuff to wrap around patient's arm would be attached here

Dial indicates blood pressure

•1897 ASPIRIN *Felix Hoffman and Hermann Dreser*

Traditional healers have often used the willow as a source of medication. In 1853, German chemist Karl Gerhardt made its active ingredient synthetically. But it wasn't until 1897 that a chemically pure, non-irritant form of the drug was isolated by researchers Hoffman and Dreser.

Aspirin tins, c.1930

Metal plates – one to attract the beam, the other to repel it

Cathode-ray tube

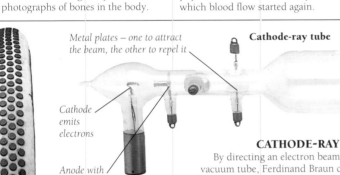

Screen coated with powder that glows when struck by the beam of electrons

Cathode emits electrons

Anode with hole to create beam of electrons

•1897 CATHODE-RAY TUBE *Ferdinand Braun*

By directing an electron beam at a fluorescent screen in a vacuum tube, Ferdinand Braun created the first cathode-ray tube in 1897. His simple tube formed a spot on the screen, which could be moved around. This discovery was crucial in the development of television, which builds up a picture by scanning the dots across a cathode-ray tube.

This taxi only has room for two passengers.

Driver sits outside on an exposed seat

Bersey electric taxi, 1897

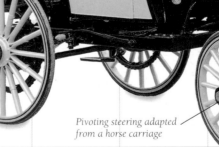

•1895 CAR PNEUMATIC TYRE
André and Edouard Michelin

Following Dunlop's patents for pneumatic (inflatable) tyres on bicycles (*see* **1845**), car manufacturers began to fit inflatable tyres to their vehicles. The French Michelin brothers made the first successful pneumatic tyres for cars, demonstrating them during a race between Bordeaux and Paris in 1895. The race was a qualified success: the brothers took 22 spare inner tubes, and they had so many punctures that they used them all! Other tyre manufacturers, such as Dunlop, soon started to mass-produce their own tyres.

Pneumatic tyre, c.1903

•1896 MOTOR TAXICAB
Germany

Taxicab passengers worldwide argued with the driver over the fare until the invention of motorized taxicabs with meters in 1896. Taxicabs, with a meter connected to the wheels, measured the distance the vehicle had travelled. They first appeared in Stuttgart, Germany, then rapidly spread to other European cities, and to the USA.

Solid wheels make rides bumpy

Pivoting steering adapted from a horse carriage

•**1895** In Europe and the USA, the most fashionable interiors were decorated in the Art Nouveau style of flowing patterns based on the forms of nature.
•**1896** In Athens, Greece, 13 countries take part in a modern Olympic Games, based on the original Olympics.

Art Nouveau motif

•**1896** Dutch scientists discover that feeding chickens on polished rice gives them a disease similar to the human disease beriberi.
•**1898** An explosion sinks a US battleship off Cuba, beginning a war between the US and Cuba's ruler, Spain. US victory follows after nearly 5 months of fighting.

•**1898** The unpopularity of foreigners in China leads to murderous attacks on them. Foreign newspapers called the violence the "Boxer Rebellion" after the groups who led them: translated into English, their name means "righteous harmony fists".

Boxer Rebellion

•**1899** In the African Transvaal and Orange Free State, war breaks out between the British and the Boers. Although the British win, the Boer War (or South Africa War) creates the modern state of South Africa.

1900

1905

| | | 1900 | 1901 | | 1904 | 1905 | 1906 | | 1908 | 1909 |

COUNTING & COMMUNICATION

•1900 SOUND MOVIE
Léon Gaumont
The problem of getting the disc gramophone and movie projector to run at the same speed was solved by Frenchman Léon Gaumont in 1900. A workable sound movie system, the Vitaphone, followed in 1927. Sound-tracked films, or talkies, were an instant success and soon killed off silent movies, the last of which was made in 1930.

Autochrome photograph of butterflies

•1903 AUTOCHROME PHOTOGRAPHY
Auguste and Louis Lumière
Practical colour photography began in 1903 when the French Lumière brothers invented autochrome photographic plates. They covered their glass plates with grains of potato starch dyed orange, green, and violet then applied a light-sensitive coating. The grains filtered the light during exposure in the camera, and tinted the picture with the correct colours on viewing.

Early Geiger counter

•1908 GEIGER COUNTER *Hans Geiger*
The Geiger counter, named after German physicist Hans Geiger, turns invisible nuclear radiation into audible clicks that can be counted automatically. It was among the first tools for measuring radioactivity.

•1906 SOUND RADIO BROADCASTING *Reginald A Fessenden*
On his first radio broadcast of sound (other than Morse code), Fessenden used a water-cooled transmitter to broadcast music, a poem, and a talk. He patented a way of modulating the radio signal so that the sound striking the microphone controlled its strength. Receivers turned the variations in the radio waves back into sound. Few heard the landmark transmission from Massachusetts, USA; home radio receivers were not sold until the 1920s.

DAILY LIFE & HEALTH

•1901 VACUUM CLEANER
Hubert Cecil Booth
After watching an unsuccessful demonstration of a hand-pumped vacuum cleaner, English engineer Booth put his linen handkerchief over his mouth and sucked dust from the carpet. The filtering effect of the fabric convinced him to experiment. His early machines sucked dust down long hoses to giant horse-drawn containers, parked outside the house.

Electric motor

Hoover Suction Sweeper, 1908

Dust collecting bag

Cylinder on which tunes were recorded

Horn

Regina Hexaphone jukebox, 1908

•1906 JUKEBOX
Automatic Machinery and Tool Company
Amazing though this may seem today, the first jukeboxes played only one tune, and that was through a tube pressed to the ear! There was a choice only at phonograph parlours, where banks of machines played different cylinders for a variety of tunes (*see* PHONOGRAPH **1877**). The first true jukebox – the John Gabel Automatic Entertainer – played a selection of 24 discs through a huge horn.

•1909 BAKELITE PLASTICS
Leo Hendrik Baekeland
Baekeland, a Belgian-American chemist, announced the world's first artificial plastic in 1909. Bakelite, as he called the plastic, was a powder that set when it was heated and pressed. It did not conduct heat or electricity, so it was a good replacement for pottery parts in electrical equipment.

AGRICULTURE & INDUSTRY

Pilot's seat and engine are positioned so that they balance one another.

Cotton fabric

Wright Flyer, 1903

Take-off and landing skid

TRAVEL & CONQUEST

•1900 ZEPPELIN *Ferdinand von Zeppelin*
The rigid-framed Zeppelin airship was named after its German inventor, Count von Zeppelin, who first built the craft. Zeppelins were used as luxury passenger ships and as military craft. Few were made after 1945 as aeroplanes were cheaper, more manoeuvrable, and generally more practical than Zeppelins.

Zeppelin

•1903 AIRCRAFT
Orville and Wilbur Wright
Americans Wilbur and Orville Wright realized that for continuous flight, their aircraft had to solve three problems: lift, control, and power. They achieved this with their craft, *Flyer*. Its first flight lasted under a minute. Pilot Orville travelled less than the length of the tourist-class cabin on today's jumbo jets. A local newspaper reporter dismissed the historic event with the words "Fifty-seven seconds, hey? If it had been 57 minutes then it might have been a news item".

•1906 HYDROFOIL *Enrico Forlanini*
George Cayley (*see* **1853**) had shown that an aircraft wing could provide lift in air, so why not water, too? The development of the hydrofoil (a boat that is raised out of the water on foils) began in earnest early in the 20th century. In 1906, Enrico Forlanini, an Italian airship designer, built a successful craft that cruised on Italy's Lake Maggiore at 38 knots (70 kph / 43 mph). Now hydrofoils run regular passenger services on many of the world's rivers.

WORLD EVENTS

| 1900–1904 | | 1905–1909 |

•**1900** The population of the world is about 1,625 million.
•**1900** Austrian Sigmund Freud publishes *The Interpretation of Dreams* and lays the foundation stone for modern psychoanalysis with his theory of the unconscious.
•**1901** Victoria, queen of Great Britain since 1837, dies.

Sigmund Freud

•**1904** Work starts on the Panama Canal. When the canal opens ten years later, it links the Pacific Ocean and the Caribbean Sea by cutting through Central America.
•**1904** A Japanese attack on Port Arthur (now Lu-Shun in Manchuria, China) starts the Russo-Japanese war. Japan wins Manchuria and Korea.

•**1905** In South Africa, the world's largest diamond is discovered. The Cullinan diamond weighs more than 620 g (21 oz), or as much as 8 hens' eggs.
•**1906** The Muslim League is established to protect the rights of Muslims in India, where most people are Hindu. The League eventually brings about the division of India, and the formation of the Muslim state of Pakistan.
•**1909** American explorer Robert Peary and his team of Inuits are probably the first people to reach the North Pole.

Robert Peary searches for the North Pole

1910

1915

1911•
AIR MAIL *India*
An aeroplane first carried mail officially in 1911 at the United Provinces Exhibition in India. Aviator Henri Pecquet flew 6,000 letters a distance of about 8 km (5 miles) in a Hummer-Sommer biplane. The first regular service was inaugurated in South West Africa, which was then a German colony, in 1914. The outbreak of World War I prevented any further development of air mail, but many nations began regular services when the war ended.

British air mail postcard, 1911

c.1914 35 MM CAMERA *Various*
Motion picture makers had been using 35 mm film since 1891, but still cameras using this format did not appear until much later. The Tourist Multiple, patented by New Yorker Paul Dietz in 1914, was probably the first. It took an incredible 15 m (50 ft) of film – enough for 750 photos. Serious photographers only began to accept the 35 mm camera with the sale of the compact Leica in the 1920s.

35 mm Leica UR camera

German Oscar Barnack modelled his successful 1925 Leica camera on this prototype, which he built 12 years earlier.

•1910 FOOD MIXER
George Schmidt and Fred Osius
The food mixer found its way into the kitchen from the American milkshake parlour. Since 1904, electric stirrers had been beating ice cream and milk into "shakes". The manufacturers, Schmidt and Osius of Wisconsin, joined with Hamilton Beach Manufacturing Company to sell an electric egg-whisk in 1910. Multi-purpose mixers were on sale from the 1930s, but the food processor is more recent (*see* **1971**).

Sundback zip fastener, 1914

Electric motor

Food mixer, 1918

Whisks

•1914 ZIP *Otto Frederick Gideon Sundback*
The story of the zip fastener began when American Whitcomb L. Judson launched "the clasp locker or unlocker for shoes" in Chicago, USA, in 1893. They were called slide fasteners and were impractical for clothing as they were prone to burst open or jam. Credit for the first practical zip belongs to Swede Otto Sundback, whose "hookless fastener" went on sale in 1914.

•1914 TRAFFIC LIGHT *American Traffic Signal Co.*
The first recorded "traffic light" guarded the entrance to Britain's Houses of Parliament from 1868 until it exploded! The first true traffic lights for regulating traffic flow on roads appeared in Cleveland, Ohio, USA in 1914. They were simple red-stop, green-go signals; the amber light was added in New York four years later.

Traffic light, c.1930

•1915 HEAT-RESISTANT GLASS
Pyrex Corning Glass Works
Heat shatters most glass because the hottest areas expand, causing powerful stresses. Heat-resistant glass, such as Pyrex, contains high levels of the mineral borax (sodium borate), which stops the expansion. Americans Eugene C. Sullivan and William C. Taylor did not invent heat-resistant glass, but it was through their work that the Pyrex Corning Glass Company was able to market the first glass cookware in 1915. The company sold flame-proof glass pots from 1936.

Pyrex advertisement

A grab line is attached to the wooden hull

Tailplane

Pilot's seat

Propeller

Water rudder

Flying boat, 1921

•1910 SEAPLANE *Henri Fabre*
French aviator Henri Fabre took off from water in 1910 astride an aircraft that looked alarmingly fragile. Other pioneers soon created sturdier seaplanes – aircraft which had floats instead of wheels – and flying boats. Today, seaplanes are mainly used in areas where it is difficult to build an airstrip, such as mountain regions.

•1916
TANK *William Tritton*
The tank – an armoured, track-laying vehicle– was a British secret weapon during World War I. Army officials called the hull a "water carrier"; workers nicknamed it "tank". The British tank that went into battle in 1916 was based on designs by William Tritton and W. G. Wilson. It lurched forward so clumsily that the crew had to wear padded clothes.

Caterpillar tread

•**1910** The ocean passenger liner *Mauretania* sails across the Atlantic in less than five days, setting a new speed record for the route.
•**1911** Revolution in China overthrows the Ch'ing dynasty, and ends 30 centuries of imperial rule. China becomes a republic, led by Yuan Shikai.

•**1914** Ethnic differences and national rivalries lead to a war in Europe, with Germany, Austria, Turkey, and Hungary fighting an alliance of Britain, France, Italy, and Russia.

German soldiers, World War I

•**1917** The USA is drawn into the European war, which has become known as the Great War.
•**1917** A revolution in Russia removes the Czar, putting a communist regime into power.
•**1918** The war in Europe (World War I) ends with German surrender. Some 10 million fighters died in it.

The Russian Revolution

•**1918** British women over the age of 30 win the right to vote after a struggle that had begun in 1867. Campaigners for women's suffrage (voting rights) are known as suffragettes.

1920

1925

| 1920 | 1921 | | 1926 | 1927 | 1928 | 1929 |

COUNTING & COMMUNICATION

1921·
LIE DETECTOR
John A. Larson
While he was a medical student at the University of California, USA, Larson studied lying by monitoring people's heartbeat and breathing. Whenever his subjects lied, their pulse and breathing became faster. By adding an electrode to monitor skin response (sweating), he created the polygraph, or lie detector. The machine is not perfect and clever liars can cheat it.

Television screen

Logie Baird televisor, 1926

•1926 BLACK AND WHITE TELEVISION *John Logie Baird*
Scottish inventor John Logie Baird demonstrated his televisor in 1926. His system could not broadcast sound and picture together, but he got round these practical problems with an excellent publicity stunt. Viewers saw famous singer Gracie Fields sing on screen – then she disappeared and they heard her song. Logie Baird's crude mechanical system, and a similar version of it developed independently by Charles Jenkens in the USA, were replaced by more successful electronic models in the 1930s.

•1928
COLOUR TELEVISION *John Logie Baird*
John Logie Baird demonstrated that his television system could also reproduce crude colour pictures. He and other inventors tried to perfect this, but solving technical problems and setting standards delayed the introduction of a working colour TV service until 1953 in the USA.

DAILY LIFE & HEALTH

•1920
HAIR DRYER *Racine Universal Motor Company*
The first purpose-made hair dryers were boxes that stood on the table; hand-held dryers were introduced by the US Racine Universal Motor Company in 1920.

•1921 INSULIN
Frederick Grant Banting and Charles Best
With the extraction of the hormone insulin from the pancreas of pigs in 1921, two Canadian biochemists at last found a treatment for the disease diabetes. Diabetics injected themselves with the pig insulin for more than 60 years, until American biochemist Michael Katsoyannis and scientists in China independently made the substance artificially in 1966.

Insulin, 1929

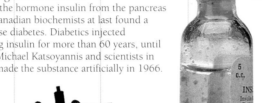

Hair dryer, 1925

1928·
ANTIBIOTICS *Alexander Fleming*
The first antibiotic drug, penicillin, was discovered by Scottish bacteriologist Alexander Fleming in 1928. However, it was only available in small quantities and was not identified as a powerful antibiotic until Ernst Chain, Edward Abraham, and Howard Florey pioneered ways of manufacturing it at Britain's Oxford University in 1939. Wounded Allied soldiers received the first samples of the drug in World War II.

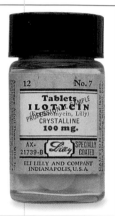

Antibiotics, 1951

AGRICULTURE & INDUSTRY

This bulldozer is clearing rubble from the streets of London after World War II

Bulldozer, 1946

c.1923
BULLDOZER *Various*
In 1885, US engineer Benjamin Holt devised a crawling tractor, which he called the Caterpillar. By the 1900s his tractors had scraping blades attached to the back and were used to move earth. The first bulldozers to be made on a large scale were produced in the USA by the LaPlant-Choate Manufacturing Company in 1923.

Robert Goddard beside his rocket, 1926

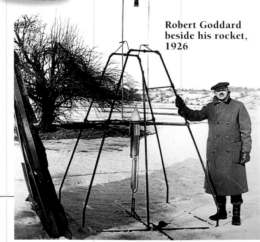

Whittle jet engine, c.1940

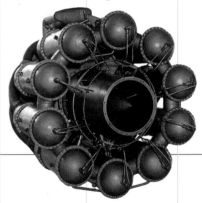

TRAVEL & CONQUEST

•1920
"TOMMY" SUBMACHINE GUN *John T. Thompson*
Many machine guns were too heavy to hand hold while firing. The submachine gun, a continuous-firing hand weapon, appeared just after World War I. One of the best-known – the tommy gun – was invented in 1920 by American army officer John T. Thompson and produced in 1921.

•1921 MOTORWAY *Germany*
The world's first motorway, the Avus Autobahn in Berlin, Germany, opened in 1921. It had been planned earlier, but World War I prevented its completion. The autobahn doubled as a race track. The design included a loop at each end so that the racing cars could whiz round without stopping.

Motorway, or autobahn, Germany

•1926
LIQUID-FUELLED ROCKET
Robert Goddard
The liquid-fuelled rocket launched by American physicist Robert Goddard in 1926 rose to only 56 m (184 ft), but it had far-reaching effects on space exploration. It was powered by supplies of petrol and liquid oxygen. Today, many space vehicles make use of this method of propulsion, but at the time, the US government did not recognize his achievements.

•1928
JET ENGINE *Frank Whittle*
Englishman Frank Whittle had the idea for the jet engine in 1928 and built a prototype in 1937. However, the first jet aircraft to fly was built in Germany by Ernst Heinkel in 1939. The designer built the aircraft with the help of information that Frank Whittle revealed in his 1930 patent application.

WORLD EVENTS

1920–1924

- **•1920** Austrian politician Adolph Hitler forms the Nazi (National Socialist German Worker's) Party.
- **•1920** Indian leader Mahatma (great soul) Gandhi promotes a campaign of peaceful civil disobedience to try and end British rule of his country.
- **•1922** The opening of a tomb in Egypt reveals the 3,000-year-old-body of King Tutankhamun. Beautiful treasures, perfectly preserved by the dry climate, surround the coffin.

- **•1924** The Ford Motor company manufactures its 10-millionth automobile.

Model T Ford

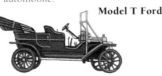

1925–1929

- **•1925** South African novelist Thomas Mofolo writes his classic romance Chaka.
- **•1926** Threatened with wage cuts, British miners go on strike. Industrial workers support them, but the general strike lacks middle-class support, and the police and army soon defeat the strikers.

Laurel and Hardy

- **•1927** In the USA, comedians Stan Laurel and Oliver Hardy make the first of many films together.
- **•1928** US aviator Amelia Earhart becomes the first female passenger on a transatlantic flight. Four years later she goes on to become the first woman to fly solo across the Atlantic from the USA to Ireland.

1930

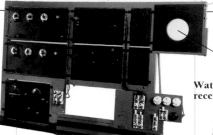

Watson-Watt radar
receiver, 1935

*Cathode-ray
tube screen*

Tape recorder,
1950s

1933–1935 RADAR
Rudolph Kühnhold, Robert Watson-Watt
Long before World War II began, Britain and
Germany worked on ways to detect enemy aircraft. Teams in both countries invented
radar (short for radio detection and ranging) at about the same time. German
Rudolph Kühnhold was the first to demonstrate (in 1933) that radio signals could
reveal ships and aircraft before they could be seen. The British team, led by Robert
Watson-Watt, was the first to build a working radar defence system in 1935.

c.1930
POP-UP TOASTER
McGraw Electric Company
Electric toasters existed at the
end of the 19th century, but
breakfast got more exciting in
the 1930s with the invention of
the pop-up toaster. Americans
who could afford the $13.50
price were the lucky ones: the
country was in the grip of an
economic depression.

•1931
ELECTRON MICROSCOPE *Ernst Ruska*
German physicist Ernst Ruska received the Nobel Prize
for his pioneering work in building a powerful
microscope. It magnified specimens by bombarding
them with tiny particles called electrons and formed
pictures on a screen like a TV. His machine magnified
only 17 times, but other researchers soon built better
models. Today, electron microscopes are vital
research tools in the laboratory and in industry.

Electron
microscope, 1936

Chrome pop-up
toaster, 1950

1933•
POLYTHENE *R.O. Gibson*
In 1933, British chemist R.O. Gibson experimented with
ethylene gas and created polyethylene, now called "polythene".
This plastic is tough, flexible, and long lasting. Its long life
causes problems: it doesn't rot away, so today's polythene
shopping bags will still be around a century from now.

Modern
version of
a cat's-eye
road stud

1934•
CAT'S-EYE ROAD STUDS *Percy Shaw*
British inventor Percy Shaw was driving in thick fog
when the eyes of a cat reflected the headlamps of
his car. He braked to avoid the cat, and only then
realized that its glowing eyes had saved his life. If
he had not stopped, he would have driven over a
cliff edge. This experience inspired him to create
road reflectors which he called "cat's-eyes". They
have since saved countless more lives.

•1931 STABILIZERS *Britain and Italy*
In 1931, experiments to stop ships from rolling showed that small
gyroscopes could be used to control the position of fins below the
waterline and stabilize the vessel. The first passenger liner with
stabilizers was the British-built Italian ship *Conte di Savoia*.

•**1930** US astronomer Clyde
Tombaugh discovers Pluto – the
9th planet in orbit round the Sun,
and the most distant from it.
•**1933** In Germany, the ruling
Nazi party begins to build
concentration camps for the
systematic killing of millions of
Jews, homosexuals, and gypsies.

Chinese troops on
the Long March

•**1934** Chinese communist troops
led by Mao Ze-dong begin the Long
March, a 10,000-km (6,000-mile)
journey on foot to escape from the
Chinese Nationalist army.
•**1936–1939** The Spanish Civil
War begins when General Franco
leads a nationalist army against the
republican government. With help

1935

•1935
TAPE RECORDER *Germany*
Magnetic sound recording began in
1898, but it was not practical
until German company I.G.
Farben produced a magnetic tape
in 1935. Soon after, the German
company, AEG Telefunken,
created a "Magnetophon" that would record on
tape and play back. During World War II,
German radio stations used the new machines
to record Hitler's speeches for later broadcast.

Light source

Paper transport

*Electric
motor*

First
automatic
photocopier,
1940

•1938 PHOTOCOPIER
Chester Carlson
American physicist and lawyer
Chester Carlson invented the
photocopier, which used static
electricity to stick black toner
particles on to copy paper in a
pattern that matched the
original document. Carlson
eventually became a
millionaire from his
invention. The first practical
copiers for office use did
not go on sale until 1960.

*This photocopy
gives the name
of the town,
Astoria, and
the date of the
experiment.*

Carlson's first
photocopy, 1939

•1934 NYLON
Wallace Hume Carothers
In 1934, W.H. Carothers led
a research team at American
chemical giant Du Pont in the
search for an artificial silk.
They found that a highly
elastic thread could be drawn
from plastic. The first product
made of nylon was a
toothbrush. Nylon stockings
were launched in 1940.

Nylon stockings

*DDT spray
emerges from
nozzle*

1939•
DDT INSECTICIDE *Paul Müller*
The world's first synthetic insecticide, DDT, was isolated
by German Othmar Zeidler in 1874. In 1939, Paul
Müller of Switzerland recognized its potential in killing
the mosquitoes that carry the disease malaria. However,
DDT also killed the wildlife that fed on
insects and in the 1970s, most
developed countries
banned it.

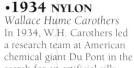

DDT pump, 1940s

*Bottle contains solution
of DDT insecticide*

*Pump atomizes and
sprays liquid DDT*

*Clock in meter
limits parking
time for each
vehicle, so that
space becomes
free for other
motorists.*

•1936 HELICOPTER *Heinrich Focke*
Model helicopters were popular from the 17th century onwards.
However, the first practical helicopter was Heinrich Focke's
Fa-61. Focke's helicopter had two rotors that turned in opposite
directions. Around the same time, Igor Sikorsky developed a
practical helicopter in the USA that used a single rotor to provide
lifting power. Most of today's helicopters are of this type.

•1935 PARKING METER *Carlton Magee*
Motorists looking for somewhere to park in a crowded
street can blame Carlton Magee of Oklahoma City, USA
who invented the parking meter in 1932. His machines
rented a few yards of kerb for a nickel an hour.

from Germany, France, and Italy, he succeeds in
defeating the republican army and takes control
of Spain in 1939.
•**1937** The second Sino-Japanese war begins as
Japanese soldiers move across China and make a
series of conquests .
•**1939** Adolph Hitler – by then Führer (supreme
leader and dictator) of Germany – orders his country's
troops to invade Poland, starting World War II.

**Republican fighters, Spanish
Civil War**

1940–2000 Transistors and the information age

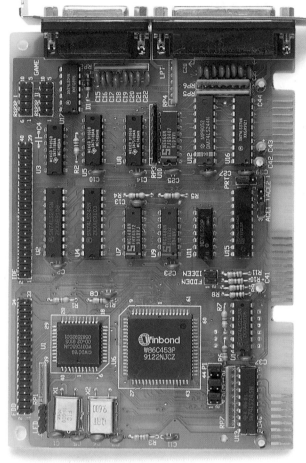

Microchips installed in a printed circuit board from a personal computer

TWO DAYS BEFORE CHRISTMAS in 1947, Walter Brattain took a razor blade and sliced across a tiny piece of gold foil. He pressed the cut edges against a chunk of germanium metal, and connected wires to the foil. "I found that if I wiggled it just right," he said later, "I had an amplifier." He had created the world's first transistor.

Brattain and his team at Bell Laboratories had been working towards this moment for months. They knew their invention would replace valves – the fragile, and unreliable glass bulbs inside the radios and other electronic devices of the time. But what they could not have understood that winter day was how completely their invention would change society. Over the next 40 years, the transistor and its successor, the integrated circuit, swept away technology that had hardly changed since the invention of steam power. It was like a second industrial revolution.

Knowledge and profit

The first industrial revolution changed for ever the way things were made, replacing skilled workers with machines that could do the same jobs more quickly and cheaply. But the transistor did not just change factories or what they manufactured, it replaced many of them with an industry that created, stored, bought, and sold *information*. Compared with creating and selling real things, such as cakes or cars, trading information is perhaps a strange idea, but it is not a new one. In the mid 19th century, one of the first applications of the electric telegraph was in news distribution. News agencies such as Reuters and Associated Press collected news from their correspondents, then used the electric telegraph to sell the information to

TRANSISTORS AND INTEGRATED CIRCUITS

The first transistors were still big enough to be wired up by hand in place of temperamental glass valves. But 40 years of development have made them unimaginably small; the maze-like pattern on the surface of an integrated circuit just the size of your thumbnail may incorporate a million or more transistors. Life today would be unthinkable without integrated circuits: a pocket calculator would be desk-sized, and a Game Boy would fill your living room.

THE CHANGING WORLD: 1940–2000

NUCLEAR ENERGY
As scientists learned more about the atom, they realized the potential of nuclear energy as a source of unlimited power to produce electricity – or in war. The threat of nuclear weapons would eventually change the face of international politics.

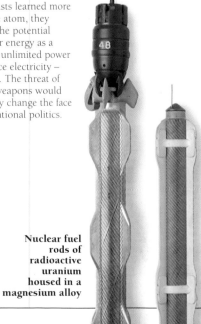

Nuclear fuel rods of radioactive uranium housed in a magnesium alloy

COMPUTERS
Today computers are used for almost everything – from medicine to administering government departments – and making this book.

CREDIT CARD
Like the bank note, the credit card has changed society. Consumers have been urged to buy on credit, fuelling industry, and encouraging everyone to carry a rolling burden or debt that keeps them working constantly.

COMMUNICATION
Television provides people with entertainment at the push of a button. Politicians quickly grasped the opinion-forming power of TV, and modern revolutionaries often storm the TV station before the president's palace. Today, satellite TV enables people all over the world to watch events, such as the Olympics, as they happen.

newspaper publishers. The transistor speeded up the collection, processing, and distribution of information – long before it replaced expensive glass valves on the circuit boards of computers.

Transistors into computers

The transistor revolutionized the computer, making it a practical, though still costly, research tool. By 1971 – just 24 years after the transistor's invention – computer technology relied on a tiny chip of silicon the size of a thumbnail. The invention of the integrated circuit would eventually put a computer on every desk.

As computers grew in power, they started to change the way people worked, and even work itself. Computer-controlled robots replaced human workers on the production line, and telephone cables linked computers so more people could work at home, travelling in to their offices only for meetings.

Faster computers have also speeded up electronic communications, blurring the boundaries between the telephone, radio, television, and computer data links. Soon urban households may use a single "data highway" to make telephone calls, pay bills, programme a video recorder, or check a train timetable.

The future with computers

Operating a computer in the 1990s is no longer a difficult task that involves setting hundreds of switches or understanding a complex language: modern computer users can simply highlight and process information on a screen by clicking a "mouse". Today, computers that can "hear" and respond to simple speech are starting to become commonplace. As computers become more and more able to understand us, we will probably find ways of communicating with them just as we communicate with each other. Eventually, we will start to use them to do jobs that we cannot yet imagine.

THE PROCESS OF INVENTION
NATIONAL AND INTERNATIONAL RESEARCH

NASA scientists at work

As technology has advanced during the 20th century, it has become much more complicated. This, in turn, has made invention (or more accurately, research and development) cost more. Since World War II (1939–1945) the largest research projects have been so expensive that no private businesses could afford them. Space research is a good example. Until very recently, only governments had enough money to build spacecraft and launch them into orbit. The USSR was the first to do this, launching Sputnik I in 1957. The USA responded by establishing the National Aeronautics and Space Administration (NASA) the following year. In 1962, NASA began a prestigious but enormously costly programme that eventually led to US astronauts walking on the moon.

MISSILE TO GAME BOY

Military research has figured prominently in the story of 20th-century invention, but its long-term effects have not always been threatening. The very first electronic computers, for example, were devised in the UK for decoding enemy radio messages in World War II. In the USA, the ENIAC computer was built to calculate the flight paths of shells, so that gunners could hit their targets with more accuracy. Both these research programmes led to great advances in civilian

computing. A major military breakthrough after the war was the invention of minute electronic components – the first integrated circuits – for guiding nuclear missiles. Today, we use descendants of these integrated circuits in tiny laptop computers, in virtual reality, and in electronic games consoles.

Using virtual reality, scientists can investigate complex molecular structures

THE JET AGE

When the huge Boeing 747, the first wide-bodied jet, entered service in 1970, many airline experts wondered whether enough passengers could ever be found to fly in it. In fact, the jumbo jet helped make air travel affordable for the first time for millions of people.

SPACE TRAVEL

The Earth is constantly circled by satellites that are able to transmit information from one side of the planet to the other.

The US space shuttle Discovery launches three satellites

ROBOTS

Since the 1970s, electronic robots have increasingly been used in place of human workers to carry out dull, repetitive jobs on the production line. Unlike people, robots are never sick, they don't take holidays, and they never strike. However, robots cannot come up with new ideas, and they cannot be laid off to save money.

GENETIC ENGINEERING

The discovery that DNA is the basic molecule of life coupled with our power to manipulate it have opened up many new horizons for research and medicine, including the possibility of eliminating many inherited diseases.

Geneticist Stanley Cohen's notebook describing the first recombinant DNA experiment.

1940

1945

| 1940 | 1941 | 1942 | 1943 | 1944 | 1945 | 1946 | 1947 | 1948 | 1949 |

COUNTING & COMMUNICATION

Spray nozzle

Aerosol can

1946•
COMPUTER *John V. Atanasoff, John Eckert, and John Mauchly*
Around 1937, John V. Atanasoff of Iowa State University built the first electronic computer, although it was never fully functional. The first successful, automatic, general-purpose electronic computer was a monster machine built at the University of Pennsylvania by Americans John Eckert and John Mauchly. Called ENIAC (short for electronic numerical integrator and calculator), its 19,000 valves used as much electricity as 200 electric fires.

ENIAC computer, 1948

Long-playing record, 1950

DAILY LIFE & HEALTH

•1941 AEROSOL CAN *Various*
A Norwegian named Erik Rotheim developed a method for dispersing liquids and powders in a spray as early as 1926, but his idea was not developed for commercial use until 1941 when two US researchers, Lyle Goodhue and William Sullivan, adapted his idea to make a spray can. After World War II, more refinements to the propellant, can, and contents created the sprays in daily use today.

1944•
PLASTIC ARTIFICIAL EYES *USA*
Glass eyes were invented in Venice, Italy in the 16th century. The more durable and realistic plastic eye is a modern invention. World War II stopped the export of glass eyes from Germany, the main producer, so a group of US manufacturers and military doctors worked together to produce an unbreakable artificial eye.

Plastic artificial eye, 1944

1946•
MICROWAVE OVEN *Percy LeBaron Spencer*
American Percy LeBaron Spencer noticed that a chocolate bar in his pocket had melted while he was standing in front of a magnetron, the electronic tube at the heart of a radar transmitter. He guessed that the microwaves generated by the tube had melted the bar. He became convinced that microwaves could be used for cooking. The first microwave ovens were patented in 1946. Home microwaves didn't appear until 1955.

1948•
LONG PLAYING RECORD
CBS Corporation, USA
With the introduction by the CBS Corporation of the unbreakable vinyl "LP" (long-playing record), the gramophone could at last rival the radio for playing longer pieces of music. The breakthrough came by making the grooves on the disc narrower, and slowing the turntable speed from 78 revolutions a minute to 33.

Home microwave oven, 1955

AGRICULTURE & INDUSTRY

•1942
NUCLEAR REACTOR *Enrico Fermi*
The world's first nuclear reactor for producing power was built at the University of Chicago, USA by Italian physicist Enrico Fermi. It was called an "atomic pile" because it was a pile of carbon blocks and radioactive uranium. The neutrons that the uranium atoms gave off as they decayed speeded the decay of other uranium atoms nearby; these gave off more neutrons. Rods in the pile absorbed neutrons, controlling the process, but when Fermi withdrew the rods, the "chain reaction" which he sought began.

Fermi's second "Chicago Pile", 1943

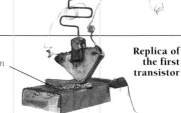

Germanium

Replica of the first transistor

•1947 TRANSISTOR
John Bardeen and Walter Brattain
A team of researchers at Bell Laboratories in the USA, led by Bardeen and Brattain, made the first transistor in 1947 with a tiny piece of a metal-like chemical called germanium. Their experimental device looks crude, but it could amplify (increase the strength of) a signal 100 times. Today, all computers and electronic devices use the same principle.

TRAVEL & CONQUEST

Mouthpiece

Compressed air cylinder

Scuba diver

•1942 MISSILE *Werner von Braun*
The first rocket-propelled missile was the surface-to-surface V-2 "Vengeance Weapon" launched as a war weapon from Germany in 1942. Rocket scientist von Braun was in charge of the team that developed it. The rocket was especially frightening because it dived towards its target faster than the speed of sound: people heard its screaming descent only after its explosion.

•1942 SCUBA
Émile Gagnon and Jacques Cousteau
Two French men perfected a self-contained underwater breathing apparatus (SCUBA) so that divers could swim at greater depths. Scuba divers strapped cylinders of compressed air, known as Aqualungs, to their backs.

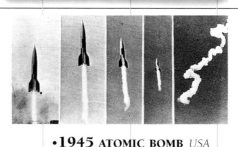

V-2 missile in flight, c.1942

•1945 ATOMIC BOMB *USA*
Throughout World War II, Great Britain and the USA worked together to produce atomic bombs. In 1945, one bomb was tested in the American desert. Later that year, two more were dropped on the Japanese cities Hiroshima and Nagasaki, killing 12,000 people.

The testing of the first atomic bomb so frightened the scientists who had created it that many of them petitioned to have nuclear weapons banned.

Atomic bomb test, USA, 1945

WORLD EVENTS

1940–1944

- •**1940** British fighter aircraft destroy many German planes, and prevent a German invasion of southern England. People call the air war the "Battle of Britain".
- •**1941** In a surprise attack, Japanese aeroplanes destroy much of the US fleet at Pearl Harbor, Hawaii. This so angers the USA that it joins the war against Japan, Italy, and Germany.
- •**1943** Dutch doctor Willem Kolff makes the first artificial kidney machine.
- •**1944** The failure of the rice crop in Bengal (now Bangladesh) causes a widespread famine in which millions starve.

Attack on Pearl Harbor

1945–1949

- •**1945** War in Europe ends in May with Hitler's suicide and Germany's surrender. World peace returns in August, after American atom bombs destroy two Japanese cities.
- •**1947** British rule of India ends. The country is divided into two independent nations. The east and west halves of a new Muslim nation – Pakistan – sandwich Hindu India. Fighting continues and, grieved by the continuing violence, Mahatma Gandhi starts a protest fast. He is assassinated the following year.
- •**1948** South Africa's National Party comes to power in a whites-only election and begins apartheid policy.

Gandhi and followers

1950

Tuning dial

Transistor radio, 1950s

1955

Circuit board with integrated circuits

1954•
TRANSISTOR RADIO *Regency Electronics, USA*
The development of the transistor (*see* **1947**) meant that electrical devices could be miniaturized. The transistor required less power, so appliances could use smaller batteries. In 1954, the first all-transistor radio, the Regency TR-1, appeared in the USA. Unlike valve radios, which took minutes to "warm-up" before the loudspeaker crackled into life, transistor radios worked as soon as you switched them on.

1956•
VIDEOTAPE
Alexander M. Pontiatoff
Pontiatoff, a Russian-born engineer working in the USA, found a way to record a TV show on a piece of magnetic tape. The first US TV show to be recorded for later broadcast was "Doug Edwards and the News" in 1956.

1959•
INTEGRATED CIRCUIT
Fairchild Semiconductor, USA
The ready-wired integrated circuits, or silicon chips, in use today were first made by Bob Noyce at Fairchild Semiconductor, although Jack Kirby of Texas Instruments had devised the theory. Noyce realized that it was possible to print an entire electronic circuit on top of a single chip, using a photographic process.

Enovid contraceptive pill, 1962

1953•
HEART-LUNG MACHINE
John Heynsham Gibbon
During open-heart surgery, a machine must pump the patient's blood. US surgeon J.H. Gibbon developed the first successful heart-lung machine during the 1930s, and he carried out the first operation on a human being in 1953.

•1954
ORAL CONTRACEPTIVE
Gregory Pincus and various researchers
US researchers showed that injecting hormones from an animal's ovaries into a rabbit controlled its fertility. Contraception (controlled fertility) for humans became practical only when artificial hormones were available. Trials of the contraceptive "pill" began in 1954.

•1957 FIBRE-OPTIC ENDOSCOPE
Basil Hirschowitz, Lawrence Curtis, and C. Wilbur Peters
To look inside the human body, doctors use an endoscope: a bendy bundle of optical fibres, each a tenth the diameter of a human hair. Most of the fibres carry images of the patient's insides to the surgeon's eye. US physician Basil Hirschowitz and physicists Curtis and Peters developed the first flexible fibre-optic endoscope in 1957.

•1950 CREDIT CARD *Ralph Schneider*
"Plastic cash" began when US oil companies issued identity cards to their customers in the late 1940s. Then, in 1950, businessman Ralph Schneider launched "The Diners Club" with the first general-purpose card for food lovers. Other businesses soon followed suit.

1956–1960
HEART PACEMAKER *Various*
With the invention of transistors in the 1950s, the pacemaker for artificially controlling heartbeat could at last be made small enough to implant under the skin.

Pacemaker, 1962

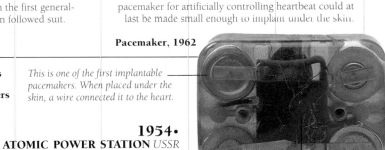

This is one of the first implantable pacemakers. When placed under the skin, a wire connected it to the heart.

Battery   Circuits

The world's first credit card – Diners Club card, c.1950

Hirschowitz's fibre-optic endoscope

Eyepiece – surgeon looks in here

1954•
ATOMIC POWER STATION *USSR*
The first real application of nuclear energy was in weapons of destruction (*see* **1945**). But harnessed for peaceful means, atomic power promised an unlimited supply of electricity. The first nuclear reactor started to produce power in 1954, and generated 5 megawatts of electricity – enough for a town of 5,000 people. Though doubts remain about their safety, today more than 400 nuclear plants produce about one-sixth of the world's power.

The world's first atomic power station at Obninsk, 1954

1957•
SPACE SATELLITE *USSR*
Most planets have satellites that orbit around them. In 1957, Soviet scientists sent the first artificial satellite into space for exploration. They used a rocket to launch into orbit a small bleeping ball, which they called Sputnik. The USA responded with a space programme that led to humans walking on the Moon 12 years later.

1959•
HOVERCRAFT
Christopher Cockerell
Looking for ways to make his craft float on a cushion of air, British boat designer Christopher Cockerell experimented with a reversed vacuum cleaner. He put a small tin inside a larger coffee tin, and blew air from the vacuum cleaner's hose into the small gap between them. Cockerell flew the first working hovercraft in 1959.

Optical fibres carry light to the tip so that the surgeon isn't working in the dark.

Edmund Hilary and Tenzing Norgay

•**1950** The population of the world is about 2,500 million.
•**1950** With the support of Russia and China, 80,000 North Korean soldiers invade South Korea. United Nations forces (comprising mostly US fighters) move to push back the attack, starting the 3-year-long Korean War.

•**1953** A team of scientists at Cambridge University discover the structure of DNA, the building block of all animal and human tissue.
•**1953** Tenzing Norgay, a Nepalese Sherpa tribesman, and Edmund Hillary, a New Zealand mountaineer, climb Mt. Everest, the world's highest peak.

Elvis Presley

•**1955** US black civil rights leader Martin Luther King leads a boycott of Alabama buses with separate seats for black and white Americans, making equal rights a national issue.
•**1956** Rock and roll music reaches the height of its popularity, bringing US rock and roll singer Elvis Presley international fame.

•**1957** Civil engineers in India finish a dam to trap the waters of the River Mahanadi. The Hirakud dam is the largest in the world
•**1958** In Britain, the Campaign for Nuclear Disarmament begins. Public rejection of nuclear weapons soon spreads from Britain to the whole world.

1960

1965

1960	1961	1962	1963	1964	1965	1966	1967	1968	1969

COUNTING & COMMUNICATION

•1962 COMMUNICATIONS SATELLITE
Bell Laboratories, USA
Soaring high above the Earth, communications satellites receive signals beamed up to them, then retransmit the signals to a receiver, sometimes on another continent, far below. In 1962, Telstar 1 was the first communications satellite to rebroadcast a television image.

Rechargeable battery in handle

Electric toothbrush, 1961

•1963 CASSETTE TAPE RECORDER
Phillips, Holland
Cassette audio tapes turned recording into a massive industry. Electronics company Phillips patented the tape cassette in 1963, but then made the design available free of charge to encourage its adoption as a world standard. Early cassette recorders had poor sound quality, and the slow tape speed created a hiss.

•1964 WORD PROCESSOR *IBM, USA*
IBM's magnetic tape selectric typewriter (MTST) was the first word processor for office use. It had no screen and its operation was primitive by today's standards. Word processors with screens appeared in the 1970s.

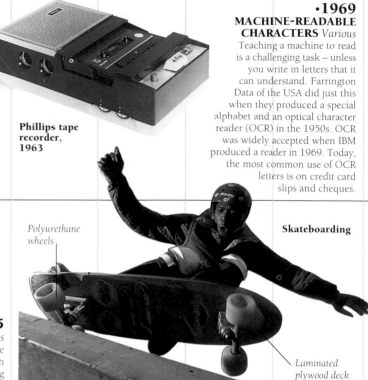

Phillips tape recorder, 1963

•1969 MACHINE-READABLE CHARACTERS *Various*
Teaching a machine to read is a challenging task – unless you write in letters that it can understand. Farrington Data of the USA did just this when they produced a special alphabet and an optical character reader (OCR) in the 1950s. OCR was widely accepted when IBM produced a reader in 1969. Today, the most common use of OCR letters is on credit card slips and cheques.

DAILY LIFE & HEALTH

•1961 ELECTRIC TOOTHBRUSH
Squibb and Co., USA
The toothbrush dates back to 15th-century China, but the world's first successful electric toothbrush was a Swiss design, made and sold in the USA. The toothbrush, named Broxodent, was launched in the USA in 1961.

c.1962 SKATEBOARD *Various*
The earliest skateboards were simply planks nailed to roller skates, so little is known of their origins. By the mid-1960s, Californian surfers were building better boards using plywood, and around 1962, the first commercial skateboards went on sale. In 1973, US surfer John Nasworthy's addition of polyurethane wheels, which were fast, silent, and shatterproof, turned skateboarding into a craze.

•1965 SCANNING ELECTRON MICROSCOPE *Various*
By scanning a beam of electrons across the surface of minute objects, scientists discovered they could achieve a very high level of magnification. The first high resolution scanning electron microscopes were developed by Charles Oatley, Dennis McMullan, and K.C.A Smith at Cambridge University, England.

Polyurethane wheels

Skateboarding

Laminated plywood deck

AGRICULTURE & INDUSTRY

Laser beam emerges through end of ruby rod

Ruby laser

•1960 LASER *Theodore Maiman*
The light that a laser produces has special qualities: the beam does not spread out, like the light from a torch; and the millions of light waves within the beam are precisely synchronized. US physicist Theodore Harold Maiman was the first to build a working laser; his machine produced a pulse of ruby-red light at the Hughes Research Laboratories in 1960. Scientists made similar devices earlier, but none produced visible light.

•1965 HOLOGRAM *Dennis Gabor*
Hungarian-born British scientist Dennis Gabor invented holography in 1948. The technique was not practical until the invention of the laser in the 1960s. With its beam, US researchers Emmet Leith and Uris Upatnieks made 3-dimensional holograms in 1965. Holograms look spectacular, but they also have practical uses: spinning holographic mirrors are used to scan a laser beam across bar codes in supermarket checkouts.

Early full-colour hologram

Vostok I

Communications aerial

TRAVEL & CONQUEST

•1961 SPACE TRAVEL *USSR*
With the launch of Soviet spacecraft Vostok I in 1961, a new era in travel began. Cosmonaut Yuri Gagarin orbited the Earth for 108 minutes in the capsule, then ejected from the spacecraft at a height of 7,000 m (23,000 ft). Although the spacecraft was controlled from the ground in case weightlessness made him unconscious, Gagarin carried a secret code that would unlock the controls if he lost contact with Earth. He never had to use it.

Gas pressure bottle for cosmonaut's life-support system

•1965 AUTOMATIC LANDING *Various*
The most dangerous part of any aircraft flight is the landing, particularly in fog. American pilot J. H. Doolittle landed a plane using on-board instruments in 1929, but blind landing like this was not safe enough for passenger flights until 1965. These systems transmit signals from radio beacons on the ground and guide approaching aircraft safely down on to the runway.

•1967 SATELLITE NAVIGATION *US Navy*
The first practical satellite navigation system, called Transit, was made in 1967 for the US Navy to help it steer ships clear of rocks and reefs. Today, with the aid of global positioning satellites (GPS), they can locate their vessels to within 100 m (328 ft) on a pocket-sized device.

First automatic landing of a scheduled airline flight at London's Heathrow airport, 1965

WORLD EVENTS

1960–1964

•**1960** White South African troops fire into a crowd of black freedom fighters, killing 69, in what becomes known as the Sharpeville massacre.
•**1961** East German authorities build a wall to divide the city of Berlin, and stop the people of communist East Germany from fleeing to the West.

The Berlin Wall

•**1962** The world is on the brink of nuclear war as the USA discovers missiles on their way to a Soviet base on the Caribbean island of Cuba.
•**1962** British pop group The Beatles have their first hit, *Love me do.*
•**1963** US president J.F. Kennedy dies of bullet wounds after being shot during a visit to Dallas.

1965–1969

•**1965** The USA begins to send more troops to Vietnam in Southeast Asia, to combat what the US government sees as the spread of communism.
•**1965** US civil rights leader Martin Luther King leads a march at Selma, Alabama in protest against black people being denied voting rights.

Martin Luther King

•**1966** Chinese leader Mao Ze-dong starts the Cultural Revolution. Red Guards (political radicals) humiliate or punish intellectuals (non-manual workers).
•**1967** In the Six-Day War, Arab countries invade Israel. Israel takes over land that it would occupy for more than 25 years.

1970

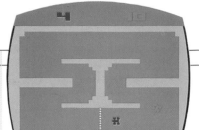

Early home video game, c.1972

1975

•**1970 FLOPPY DISK** *IBM*
Despite its rigid casing, the floppy disk really is floppy. Computer company IBM created the floppy disk for data storage, but it was microcomputers that made them popular. Earlier home computers used magnetic tape to store data; the floppy disk was far more convenient.

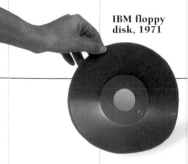

IBM floppy disk, 1971

•**1971 FOOD PROCESSOR**
Pierre Verdon
The modern food processor, invented by Pierre Verdon of France, broke completely with the traditional style of food mixers. It used a universal ring-shaped bowl for mixing, chopping, or slicing food.

•**1972 HOME VIDEO GAME** *Ralph Baer*
The world's first home video game was a simulation of table tennis called "Odyssey" invented in the USA by Ralph Baer. Two knobs on the console controlled the up-and-down movements of "paddles" (white vertical lines) on the monochrome screen. Competitors moved the paddles to keep the ball – a simple white circle – in play.

•**1972 CT SCANNER** *Godfrey Hounsfield*
While X-ray film gives a good view of dense parts of the body, such as bones, it provides poor pictures of soft tissue like the brain. So to look inside the skull, British researcher Godfrey Hounsfield developed a computerized tomography (CT) scanner. It made nearly 29,000 X-ray pictures of the brain, then spent hours analysing them. Finally, it displayed images of the patient's brain on a screen so that doctors could see a variety of angles. The subsequent introduction of whole-body CT scanners has revolutionized the way doctors examine the body.

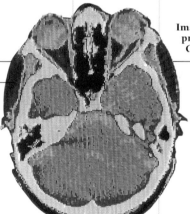

Image of a skull produced by a CT scanner

This colour-coded CT scan image shows the eyes and nose at the top, the various parts of the brain, and the bones of the skull.

Salyut 1

•**1971**
SPACE STATION *USSR*
In 1969, when US astronauts had won the race to the Moon, Soviet space scientists had begun to aim for a different goal. They planned a huge space station in orbit around the Earth, with regular "ferry" trips to change crews. The first such station, Salyut 1, was launched into orbit in 1971. The crew joined the craft later, docking with it in their Soyuz capsule.

•**1978**•
PERSONAL COMPUTER
Steve Jobs and Steve Wozniak
The first commercial personal computer, the Altair 8800, was a black box that lacked keyboard and screen. It was available in kit form in 1975. Californians Steve Jobs and Steve Wozniak created the first really successful personal computer, the Apple][, three years later. It was ready-made, and had a regular keyboard and colour screen. The two men built the first models in a garage: Wozniak sold his car to finance the venture.

Apple][personal computer

Computer and keyboard were integrated in a single box.

•**1979**
PERSONAL STEREO
Sony Corporation, Japan
The personal stereo, or "Walkman", came about as a result of reorganization at Sony. The company suddenly cut back in the tape recorder division; engineers there searched frantically for a new product to compete with other sectors. They responded with a tiny playback-only cassette recorder, and a set of lightweight headphones.

Sony Walkman, 1979

•**1974**
WAVE-POWERED GENERATOR *Stephen Salter*
Renewable sources of energy first attracted attention when war in the eastern Mediterranean region suddenly increased oil prices in 1973. More recently, environmental concerns have forced us to look again at wave and tide power. Stephen Salter of Scotland was among the first to devise a practical way of harnessing wave power in 1974.

The duck absorbs energy from the waves on the right, leaving calm water to the left.

Duck

Wave-powered generator being tested in a wave tank

•**1976 SUPERSONIC PASSENGER SERVICE** *Britain and France*
Flying at twice the speed of sound, 2,125 kph (1,320 mph), Concorde can carry up to 130 people across the Atlantic in under three hours. Britain and France agreed to build Concorde in 1962, and the prototype stretched its wings seven years later. By 1976, the world's first supersonic passenger aircraft started operating.

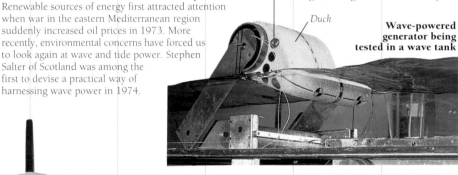

Nose of Concorde is lowered during take-off and landing to help with visibility from the cockpit

Concorde

•**1979**
CATALYTIC CONVERTER
Ricardo Consulting Engineers, England
A car's catalytic converter reduces the pollution caused by car exhaust fumes. Its high temperature turns harmful vapours and unburned fuel into water and carbon dioxide. Hot pellets of platinum act as a catalyst, making the reaction work without being used up themselves.

1970 –1974

•**1971** Swiss women are given the right to vote in elections for the first time.
•**1973** Australia's Sydney Opera House is completed after 14 years of construction. Its unusual modern design causes international controversy.
•**1973** US forces withdraw from Vietnam, ending a bloody and unpopular war. The war kills 58,000 Americans and between 35 and 50 times this number of Southeast Asian people.

Sydney Opera House

1975–1979

•**1975** In the USA, Stephen Spielberg's thriller film *Jaws* plays to packed audiences, breaking box office records.
•**1976** Riots in South Africa's black township of Soweto kill more than 250 people.
•**1976** Spain holds its first democratic elections in 41 years.
•**1976** In England, Punk Rock music begins with the formation of The Sex Pistols.

•**1978** A woman in Britain gives birth to a "test tube baby". Doctors removed one of her eggs, fertilized it with her husband's sperm, then implanted the egg in her womb to grow.
•**1979** With the overthrow of the Shah of Iran, who had ruled since 1941, the country becomes an Islamic republic, led by Ayatollah Khomeini.

1980

| 1980 | 1981 |

1985

| 1985 | 1986 | 1987 | 1989 |

COUNTING & COMMUNICATION

•1981
STILL VIDEO CAMERA
Sony Corporation, Japan
Electronic still video cameras do not use film. Instead, a magnetic disk or a memory chip stores pictures, which don't need to be processed and are ready for printing or display on a TV screen.

Sony Mavica – still video camera

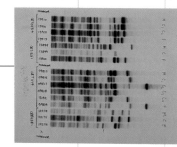

Domestic satellite receiving dish

•1983
SATELLITE TV *US Satellite Communications Inc., USA*
TV stations used to broadcast their programmes to viewers from tall antennae on the ground. Direct broadcast satellite TV became possible in 1983, when US Satellite Communications Inc. began broadcasting five channels to the area around Indianapolis, in the USA.

•1985 DESKTOP PUBLISHING
John Warnock, Paul Brainerd
With the aid of desktop publishing (DTP) software, editors and designers can create book, newspaper, and magazine pages on a personal computer screen. DTP was made possible by the combination of laser printers for sharp, high-quality print and a new software programme, called "Page-maker" (written in the USA), which specifies the shape and position of letters on the page.

•1989
GAME BOY
Nintendo, Japan
Nintendo launched this hand-held video game to create a new software market. Unlike other video games, it appealed equally to boys and girls of varying ages and it worked well on a tiny screen. Game Boy was a huge success, selling 100 million in four years; today one-third of all Japanese and American homes have one.

DAILY LIFE & HEALTH

•1980
RUBIK'S CUBE *Ernő Rubik*
This maddening puzzle was devised by a Hungarian professor. It was launched in 1980 and became an international craze. Turning the cube until each face was a uniform colour looked easy, but the game was almost impossible to do at random and had to be solved by the right combination.

•1982
ARTIFICIAL HEART
Robert K. Jarvik
In 1982, a surgeon at Utah Medical Centre, USA replaced a man's heart with a compressed-air driven artificial heart made by Robert Jarvik. The operation was a success and the heart pumped blood for 16 weeks. Today, artificial hearts are used as temporary replacements for natural hearts until a donor can be found.

Rubik's cube

DNA details – a genetic "fingerprint"

•1984
GENETIC FINGERPRINTING *Alec Jeffreys*
Just as everyone has different fingerprints, so too each of us has a unique pattern of DNA (the protein that the body uses to encode human characteristics). A British geneticist suggested that DNA patterns could be used for identification purposes. Suspected criminals can be identified by the DNA in material such as saliva or hair left at the scene of the crime.

•1987 GENE GUN *John Sanford*
Until 1988, geneticists (scientists who study heredity and variation in living organisms) aiming to introduce new genetic material into a cell to change its structure, had to use a time-consuming procedure. They combined the DNA with a virus, which carried the genetic material into the target cell, where it could multiply. John Sanford of Cornell University, USA, simplified the process by devising an instrument called a gene gun to fire the genetic material directly into the cell at high speed.

Gene gun

Jarvik artificial heart, 1985

Wind farm, USA, 1982

•1982 WIND FARM *USA*
Wind has provided power in the form of windmills for centuries, but wind turbines that generate electricity in quantity are relatively new. In 1982, the US Department of Energy built the first "wind farm", to generate more than a megawatt (one million watts). The three pylons, each with 90-m (295-ft) blades, were built at Goldendale Columbia River Gorge, in Washington State. The plant generated 2.5 MW of power.

Space Shuttle Columbia

TRAVEL & CONQUEST

•1981
RE-USABLE SPACE VEHICLE *USA*
With the launch of the Space Shuttle Columbia on 12 April 1981, the US National Air and Space Administration (NASA), achieved its objective of building a reusable space launcher. Earlier rockets were disposable: once they had lifted a satellite or some other payload, the rocket burned up in the Earth's atmosphere.

1983–1991 SMART BOMBS *USA*
The first missiles followed a straight path to the target. Cruise missiles, invented in the 1980s, are actually small pilotless planes; each carries a computerized map of the route to its target. These have led on to "smart bombs", such as the AGM-129, which follow a laser beam projected on to the target by the bomber pilot.

Stealth fighter is made using materials that soak up radar waves instead of reflecting them.

•1981 STEALTH FIGHTER *USA*
The most sophisticated of today's fighter and bomber aircraft are designed to be invisible on the radar screens of their opponents. The technology to do this is nicknamed "stealth". The first stealth aircraft, the Lockheed F-117A, flew in 1981. Special plastic materials, cool engines, and an angular arrowhead shape ensured that it did not reflect radar beams.

Lockheed F-117A stealth fighter

| 1980–1984 | 1985–1990 |

WORLD EVENTS

•**1980** The World Health Organization reveals that no cases of smallpox have been reported for five years, confirming that this killer disease has been eliminated.
•**1981** Cases of the disease AIDS are reported for the first time.
•**1984** In Ethiopia, east Africa, extensive drought damages crops

Famine in Ethiopia

causing serious famine. Thousands of people die of starvation.
•**1984** An accident at an American-owned factory releases poisonous gas into the air of Bhopal, India. The gas kills 200 people and injures 150,000 more.

•**1985** The USA starts research into a new generation of defensive space weapons to protect the country against nuclear attack.
•**1986** A reactor explodes at Chernobyl nuclear power plant in the Ukraine, causing the world's worst ever accidental release of radioactive material.

Tiananmen Square

•**1986** Halley's comet appears close to Earth again, as predicted in 1682.
•**1989** In Beijing, China, student demonstrations for greater democracy provoke violent reprisals. The army is sent in to Tiananmen Square to disperse the peaceable students.

Future trends

SATELLITE TELEPHONES *Motorola, USA*
The launch of 66 communication satellites in the near future by the US Motorola Corporation will improve worldwide communication. Named Iridium, the network of satellites will carry telephone calls anywhere in the world, without the need for telephone wires. Subscribers will use a handset that resembles a modern cellular telephone.

VIDEO TELEPHONES *British Telecom, UK*
Experiments with picture telephones began in 1927, but only now, with the development of computer data compression, are they practical. In future, higher capacity cables will improve picture quality and allow telephone companies to offer services such as films and access to information libraries.

This video phone shows the caller's face.

Video telephone

VIRTUAL REALITY *Ivan Sutherland*
US computer scientist Ivan Sutherland laid the foundations for virtual reality (VR) as early as 1965. He described his work as "…a head mounted three-dimensional display". The aim of this device was to "present the user with a perspective image that changes as he moves". The bulky helmet was based on flight simulator technology. Practical VR systems which modelled realistic scenes became possible in the early 1990s with the development of more powerful computers.

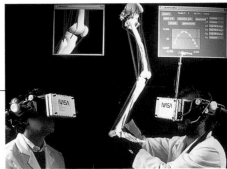

Virtual reality

VR can be used in medicine to study parts of the body in 3-D

HUMAN GENOME MAP
Progress in medicine will accelerate as the human genome mapping project reaches maturity. The aim of the project, which began in the 1980s, is to build a computer map of all the genes in the body. This genetic material defines which characteristics we pass on to our children. Geneticists hope to use this information to help cure genetic diseases – those which are passed on from one generation to the next.

Human genome mapping

VOICE RECOGNITION
Various
Pioneers, such as Marvin Minsky, began researching speech recognition in the 1960s at the Massachusetts Institute of Technology, USA, so that computers could be operated by speech. This proved impossible because understanding speech was too difficult for even the most powerful computer of the time. Researchers made progress only when they had a better understanding of language theory and began concentrating on identifying patterns and sequences of sounds. By 1994, reasonably accurate dictation systems became available, and in the future the computer keyboard may look as outdated as the abacus.

SMART CARD *Kunitaka Arimura, Roland Moreno*
The idea of giving a credit card a memory, by embedding in it a computer chip, was conceived independently by a Japanese scientist and a French journalist. In 1982, a pilot scheme started in France. Smart card-holders could use the cards to buy goods. They typed in a secure code at the till, then the cashier deducted the cost from the balance stored on the card. This trial was the model for future EFTPOS (electronic funds transfer at the point of sale) schemes.

Electronic chip

Smart card for telephone payment

SUPERCONDUCTIVITY
J. George Bednorz and K. Alex Müller of IBM, Switzerland
Since 1911, scientists have known that cooling certain materials removes all their resistance to the flow of electricity. This property of superconductivity was of little interest until the discovery in 1986 of substances that were superconductive at much higher temperatures. Superconductivity requires further research and development, but it has the potential to transform many aspects of industry and everyday life. For example, it will make computers faster and with the aid of a superconductive magnet, a train could float friction-free above the rails. Energized once at the start of the journey, the magnet would support the train without further power.

GENETIC ENGINEERING OF ANIMALS AND PLANTS
The transfer of genetic material between species may dominate progress in agriculture in the 1990s. Genetic engineering began with the work of US geneticist Stanley Cohen and biochemist Herbert Boyer. In 1973, they demonstrated that enzymes could be used to cut pieces of DNA from one organism, and the cut section spliced into the DNA of another organism, thus transferring genetic information and characteristics between species. Agricultural geneticists are now using genetic engineering to increase the milk yields of dairy cattle. In arable (plant) farming, future improvements may also be made – for example, making fruits frost-resistant.

Genetic experimentation with crops, such as this grape vine seedling, can improve their quality.

MICROENGINEERING
Using methods devised for the manufacture of integrated circuits, engineers will soon be making miniscule electric motors. These methods are already used to make sensors; for example, a tiny accelerometer triggers the release of an airbag to protect drivers when a car crashes. In future, microengineering could produce robot surgeons that will swim through our arteries and perform operations – such as the removal of blood clots – under remote control.

ZERO-EMISSION VEHICLE
Conventional petrol-driven cars cause a massive pollution problem. The clean solution shown here – the sunshine-powered car – is still at the experimental stage. The sun may eventually prove most useful as a means of "topping up" other primary power sources that engineers are now investigating. These include batteries, fuel cells, natural gas, hydrogen, and energy stored in flywheels. The US state of California leads the world in attempts to cut down car pollution, and aims to put "zero-emission vehicles" on the road in the future. These will probably run on battery power. Critics argue that such electric cars just move pollution from the motorway to the power plant that generates the cell charging current. Nevertheless, mile for mile, even a non-solar electric car creates less pollution than a conventional one.

Solar cell panels absorb sunlight and convert its energy into electricity.

Experimental solar-powered car

Index of inventions

Index of inventors

Acknowledgements

Dorling Kindersley would like to thank:
The staff of the British Museum, Science Museum, and Glasgow Museums; Esther Labi for editorial assistance; Sophie Stirling, Clare Archer for design assistance; Lynn Bresler for the index. Thanks also to the following companies for help with research: Acco-Rexel Ltd, Black and Decker Corp., Bristol-Myers Squibb, Coca-Cola & Schweppes, International Maritime Satellite Organization (Inmarsat), Iridium Inc, Konica UK, Robert Bosch LTD, Tate & Lyle, Volvo.

Key: l=left r= right c=centre t=top b=bottom a=above

Special Photography: Douglas Gowan for photography at Museum of Childhood, Beaumaris, Gwynedd 27cra. Ellen Howden and Maureen Kinnear for photography at the Glasgow Museums front cover tr;cra; 22b;bc;23cbl;24-25b;52t;56tr. Mark Gulezian/QuickSilver Photographers for photography at the Smithsonian Institution, Washington, D.C. 1;2;3;5b;24tr;27cr;31br;31tr;32cra;33cl; 34clb;cr;31br 35cla;cl;cr;crb;36cb;37cla;cra;clb;tr;38c;40cl;41cra; cr;cla;44tr;45tr;cla;crb;46crb;47tl;tr;49cra;50cla;ca;51c;52ca;cra; 53tr;cr;crb;cl;55br;56tl;cla;c;57tl;tr;ca;58tl;60c;crb;back cover tr,cr.
Additional Photography: Ashmolean Museum;British Library;British Museum;Museum of London;National Maritime Museum;National Motor Museum, Beaulieu;Pitt Rivers Museum, Oxford;Science Museum.

Photographers: Peter Anderson;Martin Cameron;Andy Crawford;Geoff Dann;Philip Dowell;Mike Dunning; David Exton;Steve Gorton;Christi Graham;Peter Hayman;John Hesiltine;Chas Howson;Dave King;Liz McAulay;Andrew McRobb;Nick Nichols;Tim Ridley;James Stevenson;Karl Shone;Clive Streeter.
Illustrators: All illustrations by Russell Barnett except for those by Nick Shewring 8bl;br;10bl;br;11bl;12bl;13bc;br;14bl;br;15bl;17br; 19bl;22bl; 23bl;br;24bl;br;25bl;br;26bl;br;27bl;34bl;35br;41bl;45bl; br;47br;48bl;49bc;50bl;br;52bl;br;53br;56bl;57bl;br;58bl and Peter Visscher 58br;59bc.
Picture Credits: Lesley and Roy Adkins Picture Library 15ca. Ancient Art and Architecture 17cl. Bank of England 2cla. Bodleian Library 14br;22tl. Bridgeman Art Library 19tr;20bl;21cb;22tc;23ccr/British Library, London 7crb;18clb;20clb/British Museum 6br. B.T.Pictures 61cla. British Dental Association 14tcr;29tc. British Museum 17tl;22tr. Jean-Loup Charmet 35tr. Christie's Colour Library 21bl. Colorsport 54br. Diners Club 57cl. C.M. Dixon 15clb. Mary Evans Picture Library 18bc;20br;25crb;26bcl;28crb;29crb;30br;31bl;31cr;33tl;33tr; 40cra;crb. E.T.Archives/Bibliotheque Nationale, Paris 21cr./British Museum14tcl/British Library 18tl/Turkish and Islamic Art Museum, Istanbul 19cb/Victoria and Albert Museum 21tr. Fitzroy-Atari 59tc. Genesis Space Photo Library 58cb. Giraudon/Vatican, Rome 20crb. Glasgow Museums 30tr;39c. Guildhall Library/Worshipful Company of

Makers of Playing Cards 27crb. Sonia Halliday 16tc;19tl. Robert Harding/Bildagentur Schuster/Schenk 8cr. Hulton-Deutsch Picture Library 30bc;41clb;42cr;bl;crb;43tr;cr;51cra;52ccl;56crb;cb;58crb. IBM Archives, New York 43cb. IBM, UK 59tl. Image Select 15tl;18cla;cr;31cr; 34cl;38tr;39tl;crb;41tl;crb;44crb. Leica Camera Ltd 51tr. Tim Leighton-Boyce 58tcr. Mansell 12tr;13trc;15tc;23crb;cr;24cb;29cla;50clb. MARS 51crb. Military Picture Library 60crb. Motorola front cover br;61tl. Museum of London 17ca. NASA 55br;tr;60clb. National Maritime Museum 24clb. National Motor Museum, Beaulieu 49crb. National Postal Museum, London 37tl. Peter Newark 8-9t. J.W. Northend Ltd, Sheffield 28clb. Novosti 57cb. Robert Opie 40tr;40ca;43br;44cla;44cl;51cr;back cover br. Philips 58tr. Popperfoto 52cb;53cb. Post Office Archives 51tl. The Royal Aeronautical Society 44clb. The Royal College of Music 26r. The Royal Photographic Society 40tl;44tl;50tl. Graham Saxby/ P. Harinaran 58cr. Science Museum 35tl;41tr;52cr;53ca;tl;back cover tc. Science Photo Library/Argonne National Laboratory 56cl;/Martin Bond 59crb;/Peter Menzel 60cb;61tc;/Hank Morgan 61tr;/Larry Mulverhill 54clb;/NASA 52ccr;/Ohio Nucleur Corporation 59cb;/Peter Pailley 61c;clb;/D.Parker 60cra;/J.Stevenson 60tc;/Geoff Tompkinson 55cr. Smithsonian Institution 31cb;43clb;56tc;59ca. Sony 59cra;60tl. Tony Stone/Mark Segal 55bl. Sygma 56crb. Texas Instruments 57tr. York Archaeological Trust 16br. Wellcome Institute Library, London 43 bl. ZEFA/Kalt 55clb.